Career Launcher

Fashion

Career Launcher series

Career Launcher

Fashion

Monique Vescia

Ferguson Publishing
An imprint of Infobase Publishing

Career Launcher: **Fashion**

Copyright © 2011 by Infobase Publishing, Inc.

Ferguson
An imprint of Infobase Publishing
132 West 31st Street
New York NY 10001

Library of Congress Cataloging-in-Publication Data

Vescia, Monique.
    Fashion / Monique Vescia ; foreword by Kevin Harter.
        p. cm. — (Career launcher)
    Includes bibliographical references and index.
    ISBN-13: 978-0-8160-7965-0 (hardcover : alk. paper)
    ISBN-10: 0-8160-7965-X (hardcover : alk. paper)
1. Fashion—Vocational guidance—Juvenile literature. 2. Clothing trade—Vocational guidance—Juvenile literature. I. Title.
    TT507.V39 2010
    746.9'2023—dc22

                                                              2009051275

Ferguson books are available at special discounts when purchased in bulk quantities for businesses, associations, institutions, or sales promotions. Please call our Special Sales Department in New York at (212) 967-8800 or (800) 322-8755.

You can find Ferguson on the World Wide Web at http://www.fergpubco.com

Produced by Print Matters, Inc.
Text design by A Good Thing, Inc.
Cover design by Takeshi Takahashi
Cover printed by Art Print Company, Taylor, PA
Book printed and bound by Maple Press, York, PA
Date printed: November 2010

Printed in the United States of America

10 9 8 7 6 5 4 3 2 1

Contents

Foreword

I have pretty much spent my whole career at Bloomingdale's. It was an accident, to be honest. I had moved to Chicago right after college, and Bloomingdale's was opening a store, and I was not quite sure what I was going to do. I applied to be a sales associate at Bloomingdale's, until I figured it out. They opened in September of 1988. I came in thinking it was a very temporary job, and a few months later they asked me to go into the management training program. The rest is history.

Right now at Bloomingdale's you choose a store line path or a buying path. But I started off in the stores, and became a department manager. They brought me to New York as a senior assistant buyer, and after about nine months they made me a buyer. I was in the buying office for a number of years, and then about 10 years ago they moved me into the fashion office.

My buying experience was valuable to my career—to becoming a fashion director—because it made me understand more of the business aspects of retail, and I could sympathize with the buyers and what they were going through. Much of my job right now is going out and finding new resources and finding great trends, and pushing that on the buyers to take advantage of those opportunities. I am able to put myself in their shoes a little bit more.

I have had two great mentors at Bloomingdale's. One of them is still one of my bosses, David Fisher, and he is the general merchandising manager, the GMM. I have worked for him for 15 years, and he is amazing. He taught me that fashion is always changing and retail has to be fun, but there has got to be balance between the fashion and the commerce. He loves creativity and loves taking risks, so he has been a terrific mentor. And the other one is Kal Ruttenstein. I had the great fortune of working for him for years before he passed away. He is the one who really taught me to find fashion and trends in unexpected places. You can go to runway shows and see some good things, but he always believed that what you spotted on the street was more important. The common thread between both Fisher and Ruttenstein is an incredible passion for retail and fashion. If you are going to be successful, you need to have a passion for this business.

In a funny way the recession of 2008–2009 impacted my work in a lot of positive ways. It was tough from the standpoint that there are fewer people. But as for my team and myself, it helped us think outside the box more and think of great ideas. It challenged us. We are out there looking for different resources. How do you find great fashion for your customer but still at a value? It is changing the way that my entire team does our job right now. I feel like we are working harder, but there is a lot of fun added to it because you are thinking outside the box a little bit.

I do a lot of traveling. I am probably on the road at least two to three months out of the year. Not only as a fashion director, but also as a buyer I have had the good fortune of seeing a lot of great places. You can find inspiration anywhere, whether it is downtown or sitting outside of a restaurant. You do not have to travel the globe. Years ago when I was just starting off, we would go sample shopping in Europe. Thanks to the Internet you do not have to travel as much, but it is important to put yourself out there in different places, whether locally or globally. Each urban area has its own beat, its own personality. That is one of the challenges of retail. How do you market to those different locations?

The Internet will continue to play a bigger and bigger role in our lives, and Internet retailing is going to become much more important. With all that is going on, people want simpler lives. They want entertainment in stores, but they also want their lives to be easier. So I think more people are going to turn to the Internet to buy their clothes. And I think it is going to be a long time before people embrace luxury as much as they did over the first few years of the century. Retailers have the opportunity to get their numbers back, but I think it is going to be with different categories. Home buying is going to become more important because people want their homes to be comfortable. You are going to see more people buy clothes that they can wear a little more easily. Still stylish, but not as stiff—I call it stylish ease. I think you are going to see people save more money, but people are still going to buy things that make them happy. It is important that retailers have a balance—there are great investment pieces that consumers are going to keep in their wardrobes for a long time, but you have still got to provide them with fashion.

Everyone who works in fashion knows that it is ever-changing. Every time I interview someone I let them know right off, if you need structure, this is not a good job for you. No two days are ever alike. And you always have to be ahead of your consumer.

Kevin Harter
VICE PRESIDENT OF FASHION DIRECTION FOR MEN'S, HOME, AND DOT-COM
BLOOMINGDALE'S, NEW YORK, NY

Acknowledgments

Many people helped send this book down the runway:
I am grateful to Kevin Harter for sharing his experiences at
Bloomingdale's, and to Helena Gubelman for bearing up under
an onslaught of nagging e-mails from me. Fashionable women
who found time in their busy schedules to talk to me include
Patricia Nugent, Edie Huntington, Leslie Jenks, and Greta Earnest.
Penny Earnest and Kamie Chang Kahlo of adelitastyle contributed,
as well. Thanks to Colleen Vescia for moving out of the "snore
bunker" so I had a place to write, and to Fernando Vescia for giving
up his study and his incredibly squeaky desk chair. A project like
this is always easier when you work with skillful and understanding people like Jeff Galas and Richard Rothschild. Finally, domestic
support was provided, as always, by Don Rauf, Leo, and Hoolie.

Introduction

This book was written during a period of upheaval in the fashion industry. Jobs were being cut, businesses were going bankrupt, and the trade papers were full of gloomy predictions about the future of the fashion industry. But in a dynamic, ever-changing field like the fashion business it pays to remember that these kinds of economic crises have happened many times before. One book I read in preparation for writing this one, *The Fashion Cycle* by Irene Daria, was published in the aftermath of the 1987 economic crash, and in many instances it reads like it was written yesterday. In her introduction, Daria writes:

> Since fashion reflects the time during which it was created, no discussion of a season would be complete without a look at the economic, social, and fashion trends that immediately preceded it. For all practical purposes, the gilded eighties, the party-till-you-drop decade, ended when the stock market crashed on October 19, 1987.
>
> Immediately before the crash, the couturier of choice was Christian Lacroix, whose clothes were perfect for the big-money, big-spending mood of early 1987....
>
> In early 1988, however, other American women began publicly questioning the absurd appearance of Lacroix's clothes, as well as their high prices. ... The same month, a column in the *New York Times Magazine* asked, "What would you rather have? A Christian Lacroix pouf or the down payment on a one-bedroom in Tudor City?" ...
>
> By June, Ivana Trump, who in March had bought a $25,000 Christian Lacroix suit, announced that Parisian clothes were just too expensive, and from now on she was buying from the significantly cheaper American knockoff artist Victor Costa.

As I researched *Career Launcher: Fashion Industry*, headlines in the fashion press were sounding the very same notes: *Recessionistas and the New Frugality; Is This the Death of Haute Couture?; Even Christian Dior Feels the Economy's Wrath*. Sixty years before, after the privations and shortages of World War II, critics were decrying the frivolity and extravagance of Dior's New Look. As always, history repeats itself, and as a result it has much to teach us.

The fashion industry constantly reinvents itself, and like the beautifully constructed hemlines it sends down the runways of the world every season, it has its downs and ups. While the specific styles that crowd the racks of department stores today will be long gone by the time you crack these pages searching for some sage advice about how to climb the fashion career ladder, my hope is that I have captured some of the essential qualities of the industry that will be of use to anyone seeking to make their way in this fascinating, creative, and dynamic business.

This book begins with a look at the industry's history (Chapter 1) and examines how a business that was started by a few forward-thinking entrepreneurs in the nineteenth century swiftly burgeoned into the huge and complex industry that employs millions of people today. Chapter 2, "The State of the Industry," offers the reader an overview of the fashion business at the beginning of the new millennium. It introduces the key players and major forces at work in the industry and supplies the most current information available on employment, wages, and profits. In Chapter 3, an alphabetical listing of key fashion jobs is grouped under the larger categories of fashion production design, merchandising and marketing, and media and promotions. Job descriptions emphasize the specific skills and preparation required for each position as well as typical paths for advancement in the industry. Chapter 4, "Tips for Success," offers specific advice on how to distinguish yourself in your current position, how to recognize and exploit opportunities for advancement, and suggestions for job hunting and interviewing for fashion jobs. Chapter 5, "Talk Like a Pro," is an extensive glossary of industry terms, from *accessory* to *zori*. Finally, Chapter 6 offers an annotated selection of fashion-related books and periodicals, listings of useful Web sites and favorite fashion blogs, and information about the top fashion schools, online programs, and relevant films.

To write this book, I tracked down interesting people working in the fashion industry and got them to tell me how they made it. How did they get their start? Was their career path straight, or as meandering as a poorly stitched seam? What did they learn from their mentors, and what would they want to teach someone new to the industry? What do they really wish they had known when they were just starting out?

I found these successful, articulate, and interesting people by networking, using my connections, just like you will have to do to succeed in the fashion industry. A college friend of mine works in the human resources department at Bloomingdale's in New York—she put me in touch with Kevin Harter, who provided the foreword for this book. An old high school friend of mine resurfaced one day in my e-mail inbox, and as we chatted I learned that she was a sales rep for the handbag designer Vera Bradley. Other useful connections I owe to a neighbor, who has a wide-ranging history in the industry and an astonishing collection of textiles; she put me in touch with a friend of hers who is an executive recruiter in the business. My networking lead me to these and other people working in the industry, who were kind enough to set aside time in their busy schedules to speak with me.

That is exactly the kind of networking you will have to do if you are serious about finding a rewarding and well-paying job in fashion. You will also need to research career possibilities and fully inform yourself about the business today as well as its history. In preparing this guide I read dozens of books about the industry (check out Chapter 6 for a list of worthwhile ones), leafed through tons of glossy magazines, and visited many Web sites and fashion blogs. I watched hours and hours of *Project Runway* and *America's Next Top Model* (OK, that was the easy part), and visited the Costume Institute at the Metropolitan Museum of Art.

Bottom line: What I learned is that the fashion industry is changing as fast as fashion itself changes, which means that new opportunities are being created every day. That is great news for the smart and resourceful individual willing to make the best use of every connection and do the research and preparation required for the job search. Change equals opportunity—make that your mantra.

In this environment, the fact that you may be fairly new to the fashion business will probably work in your favor. Relative newcomers to the industry have the advantage of not being encumbered by fixed ideas and assumptions about how things used to be (in the "good old days") and how things should be. No two career paths in fashion are ever exactly alike—there is no strict formula for achieving a certain position—for instance, one might think that in order to be a fashion editor one needs to be a skilled writer, but this is not necessarily true. You are most likely in this business because you are a creative person, and you will need to think creatively about how to approach your job search.

Tim Gunn, the *Project Runway* style guru and chief creative officer for Liz Claiborne, has said that the fashion industry really tests how badly you want to be in it—because it does not tolerate sub-par efforts. So, if you want it badly enough, it is time to get serious about your career in fashion!

Chapter 1

Industry History

Unlike other professions that were well established in the ancient world, such as medicine or law, the fashion industry as we know it is a fairly recent development in human history. Prior to the 1850s, most people either sewed their own clothes or paid a seamstress or tailor to make them. By the end of the 1860s, in the United States, a garment industry had developed to the extent that Americans were able to buy most of their clothing rather than making it themselves. In the mere 150 years or so since the designer Charles Frederick Worth opened the very first *maison de couture*, the fashion business has expanded into a multibillion-dollar global industry that, as of 2009, accounted for more than four million jobs in the United States alone. Like fashion itself, where trends come and go in the blink of an eye and every season brings a whole range of new looks, the industry has a history of rapid change. With the advent of new media and technologies, this is even truer today.

The fashion industry is a highly complex machine in part because what it produces is more than simply a commodity. What began as a means to address a basic need—to clothe the body, for warmth and protection—has evolved into an elaborate system of both cultural and individual expression and an art form in its own right. Anyone who visits the Metropolitan Museum of Art in New York City and views the extraordinary garments on display in their Costume Institute collection—a gown by Madame Grès, an opera coat by Paul Poiret—can testify to that. Today, the most successful fashion designers have become household names and celebrities in their own right, but their fame is made possible by a multitude of workers laboring in all aspects of the industry, from development and production, to merchandising and marketing, to media and promotions, and beyond. As Fern Mallis, Senior Vice President of IMG Fashion, has said, "For every Donna Karan on a label, there are thousands of people who are working to make it happen."

The fashion industry is Janus-faced—forever looking backward into its own past at the same time that it looks toward the future. Even the most forward-thinking designers reference the past in their work—in the cut of a sleeve, the choice of a fabric, the length of a hemline. Anyone who is committed to having a future in the fashion business needs to have a solid understanding of its past.

Everyone Knows

A Moral Issue

It is no secret that the American cotton industry was built on the backs of slaves. Slavery in the United States was officially abolished in 1865, but sharecroppers and migrant workers continued this backbreaking work for low wages with no benefits. Cotton is currently grown in 17 states in the southern United States, but the bulk of the cotton used in apparel manufacturing today comes from China and India, as well as smaller countries such as Uzbekistan. In all of these places, workers—some as young as 11 years old—work long hours to bring in the cotton harvest. Many are held in a condition of virtual slavery called "debt bondage," where they must work to pay back cash advances from plantation owners. Organizations such as the ILRF (International Labor Rights Forum) strive to expose labor conditions in these countries, call attention to human rights abuses, and pressure retailers to boycott products that rely on underage and underpaid labor. Leading U.S. and European clothing retailers, including giants such as Wal-Mart, The Gap, and Target, have agreed to boycott products known to contain Uzbek cotton, the harvest of which currently depends upon the forced labor of 2.7 million children.

Origins of the Fashion Industry

Human beings began wearing clothing sometime between 100,000 and 500,000 years ago, according to anthropologists. For most of that time, the making of garments was a labor-intensive process, and the majority of people either made their own clothing or paid someone else to make it for them. Before textile production was mechanized in the eighteenth century, animal and plant fibers had to be spun into thread and yarn by hand, and material such as linen and wool was hand-woven.

Fashion, as we understand it today, is a far more recent development. Cultural historians believe that the emergence of fashion dates from the mid-fourteenth century in Europe—before that time, clothing styles in Europe and elsewhere were very simple and uniform, and often remained unchanged for centuries. Paintings on the walls of Egyptian tombs that date from thousands of years apart show people (at least the wealthy ones) clad in the same translucent, pleated linen garments from one dynasty to the next. The Italian Renaissance saw the beginning of tailoring, featuring curved seams that helped fit clothing more closely to the body than allowed by the draped garments and straight seaming of previous centuries. Though the term "tailor" (i.e., one who makes clothes) dates back to the thirteenth century, the notion of a "fashion designer" in the contemporary sense did not exist before 1858.

The First Designers

The following early designers helped define fashion as both a trade and an art form, while pointing the way towards its future possibilities.

The House of Worth

Designers like Madame Demorest (a nineteenth century milliner and dressmaker widely credited with inventing mass-produced tissue-paper dressmaking patterns) and everyday tailors were not considered artists until Charles Frederick Worth (1826–1895) came along. The so-called "father of haute couture" was born in England but relocated to Paris when he was 19, where he found work at Gagelin, a firm that sold textiles and ready-made garments. The first real fashion designer, or *couturier*, Worth decided to open his own *maison de couture* when dresses he had designed for his fiancée attracted attention among upper-class women. The House of Worth was established in Paris in 1858. Worth was the first person to sew his own label into the garments that he designed; he also invented the fashion show, since up until that time dress designs were displayed on dolls, whether small or life-sized, rather than on live models. His entirely hand-sewn creations were constructed from sumptuous fabrics, with lavish embellishments, and were impeccably fitted to his clients' measurements. Worth made formal dresses for Empress Eugénie, wife of Napoleon III. In 1866, Worth was invited to create a wedding dress for Alexandria, Princess of Wales. He used the opportunity to create a new silhouette—featuring a narrower skirt with a bustle back—that changed the direction of fashion for the next three decades.

One of many haute couture designers to recognize the potential of the American market, Worth also created gowns for wealthy clients such as the American Rothschilds and the Vanderbilts. His gowns were shipped to department stores such as Sears, Roebuck and Montgomery Ward, where they were copied at in-house workshops and sold to well-heeled Americans. Worth's creations gained further exposure when they were worn on European tours by famous stage performers such as Sarah Bernhardt, Jenny Lind, and Lillie Langtry. Langtry purchased enough Worth gowns to fill 22 trunks with her touring wardrobe. Worth's salon was so successful that by 1870 he was employing 1,200 workers. After his death in 1895, Worth's two sons, Jean-Pierre and Gaston, took over the business, which passed through four generations before it was taken over by the House of Paquin in 1954.

Paul Poiret

Another important French designer from this period was Paul Poiret (1879–1944), an apprentice of both Jacques Doucet and Worth, who launched his own *maison de couture* in 1903. Poiret's innovation of the uncorseted silhouette shifted the focus in garment construction from tailoring to draping. An exhibit in the Costume Institute at the Metropolitan Museum of Art, where a selection of Poiret's garments are housed, shows how the designer created one coat by artfully draping a single piece of fabric. Poiret also introduced the notorious "hobble skirt," which was full at the hips and extremely narrow at the ankles, requiring women to walk with tiny, mincing steps. In reference to his designs, Poiret once declared, "I freed the bust but I shackled the legs."

Known for his love of strong colors, exotic shapes and details, and his exuberant theatricality, Poiret was inspired by the costumes for the Ballets Russes production of *Scheherazade* and threw lavish Oriental garden parties where his guests would appear in his latest designs, such as lampshade tunics and harem trousers. His signature was the rose, a symbol he had embroidered into his most exquisite creations. Poiret also created the very first designer perfume: He named it Rosine, after his eldest daughter, and he designed the bottles himself.

In 1927, a critic in the *New Yorker* wrote that Poiret was one to "steal ideas from the future and force them on his [own] generation." Ultimately, Poiret was a victim of fashion's fickle nature. His creations suddenly looked surprisingly dowdy next to the sleek, well-constructed silhouettes that Gabrielle Chanel was becoming famous for, and his designs fell out of style. The former self-proclaimed "King of Fashion" died poor in 1944 in German-occupied Paris.

Madame Paquin

Jeanne Paquin (1869–1936) was the first woman to become a leading fashion designer. She opened her own *maison de couture* in 1891 next to the House of Worth, and later became the first Parisian couturier to open branches in London, Buenos Aires, and Madrid. Paquin used publicity stunts to promote her designs, such as dressing all her models alike and sending them to the races or the opera. Madame Paquin was the first woman designer to be awarded the Legion d'Honneur, and she served as the first female president of the Chambre Syndicale de la Couture (the organization that regulates haute couture in France) from 1917 to 1919.

Madeleine Vionnet and the Bias Cut

In the 1920s, the French designer (interestingly, she preferred to call herself a dressmaker) Madeleine Vionnet (1876–1975) popularized the "bias cut": the practice of cutting diagonally across the weave of the fabric, which makes the material cling to the body. (While Vionnet is often referred to as "the queen of the bias cut," she did not, in fact, invent this method of cutting fabric. Dressmakers in the nineteenth century sometimes laid pattern pieces on fabric at an oblique angle, to be cut on the bias and hung this way on the body. Vionnet herself never claimed to have originated this technique.) Vionnet's innovative use of the bias cute, and the styles that she pioneered using this technique, celebrate the unconfined female form. Perhaps as a reflection of her desire to loosen the constrictions to which women had historically been subject, Vionnet used barefoot models to present her first solo collection. Vionnet designs that have become fashion staples include the halter top, cowl neck, and handkerchief dress. Her dresses showed off a woman's shape without confining the body or falsely accentuating its contours. Vionnet made use of fabrics that were rare in the apparel of the 1920s and 1930s: crepe de chine, gabardine, and satin. In her 20-year career, she created over 12,000 garments.

Mechanization of the Apparel Industry

The haute couture industry that the first true designers helped create depended on traditional dressmaking and tailoring skills and catered to a very exclusive and wealthy clientele. Prior to that, as a result of many mechanical inventions invented in the eighteenth century, a garment industry had grown up to clothe the rest of the population.

During the Industrial Revolution, advances in textile machinery such as the invention of the flying shuttle (1733), the spinning jenny (1764), the power loom (1785), and the cotton gin (1794) made it possible to replace human workers with machines and to accomplish certain time-consuming tasks far more quickly. For example, prior to the invention of the cotton gin, the sticky cottonseed had to be manually separated from the raw cotton fibers, a difficult process that took hundreds of hours. Eli Whitney's cotton gin revolutionized the cotton industry, and today American cotton production is almost entirely mechanized.

In 1846, American inventor Elias Howe patented the first sewing machine. Howe's machine was powered by a hand crank, which required the operator to stop work at intervals to crank it up. New Yorker Isaac Singer improved upon Howe's design when he devised, in the 1850s, a machine powered with a foot treadle, leaving the worker's hands free to feed the fabric toward the mechanized needle as it moved up and down. Thanks to this laborsaving device, a shirt that might have taken 14 hours to assemble and sew by hand could be made in less than an hour and a half. Initially Singer's machines were made for industrial use, but soon I.M. Singer & Co. began making smaller machines for use in the home.

Around this time, an American dressmaker and milliner named Ellen Demorest invented tissue-paper patterns as well as a mathematical system for grading patterns, or producing one pattern in a range of sizes. Customers who bought Madame Demorest's patterns could reproduce at home the same designs that they admired in the illustrated fashion magazines of the day. Soon after Demorest's innovation, clothing sizes became standardized for the first time. All these improvements made it possible to produce factory-made garments in various sizes that people could purchase at one of the new department stores established during the nineteenth century.

The Rise of Retail and the First Department Stores

The first factory-made garments were poorly made from cheap materials—such as garments for sailors to replenish their clothing quickly during their brief stops in port. The shoddy workmanship on these clothes, called "slops," was notorious and gave rise to the term *sloppy*. The first well-made ready-made clothing appeared in 1824 at the Parisian department store La Jardinière. American merchants such as R. H. Macy and Alexander Turney Stewart had recognized that there was plenty of money to be made by consolidating many smaller specialty shops under one large roof. Monsieur Bouçicault, owner of another early Paris retailer, the Bon Marché, instituted innovations that have become permanent fixtures of the retail system, such as fixed prices (before this time, prices were established through bargaining.) For the first time, clients could inspect the goods on display without any obligation to buy them, and if they were unhappy with their purchase, a refund could be arranged. Establishments like the Bon Marché stocked a wide variety of goods and targeted a range of social classes. In 1872, Japanese department stores such as Isetan and Mitsukoshi in Tokyo and Takashimaya in Kyobashi sent out catalogs of their wares to exclusive buyers and advertised their summer clearance sales with advertising inserts in newspapers of the type still in use today. American stores also made their inventories available to customers through catalogs such as the Sears, Roebuck and Co.'s "Wish Book." For the first time, people who lived in rural areas and did not have access to department stores could (if they could afford it) dress in the same styles and fashions as their city cousins.

Many American department stores opened their doors in the nineteenth century. In New York City, Lord and Taylor's began as a dry goods store in 1826, and Macy's in Herald Square opened in 1902. In 1903, Wanamaker's grandest emporium opened in Philadelphia. Marshall Field's (originally Field and Leiter) opened its doors in Chicago in 1868 and dazzled shoppers with its expensive merchandise, such as imported china and lace tablecloths. In 1907, Marshall Field & Co. moved into an eleven-story building, crowned with a Tiffany-glass dome, that occupied an entire block on State Street. The first American department store to have a European buying office (in Manchester, England), Field's was also the first such establishment to offer a bridal registry and to open a restaurant within its confines, so that the shopping experience could extend into an all-day affair.

The 1920s saw the proliferation of chain stores (first called "multiple stores") that began to rival the supremacy of large department stores in the business of fashion merchandising. These chain stores, such as Marks & Spencer in the United Kingdom, were aimed at an increasingly more prosperous working class that wanted well-made and stylish apparel but could not afford the top-quality merchandise sold in department stores.

Changing Times and Changing Fashions

Fashion and the fashion industry have always responded to larger cultural shifts. One of the most important factors in shaping the direction of fashion has been the evolving role of women in society. Confining fashions such as the tightly corseted S-bend silhouette, considered the height of fashion at the end of the nineteenth century, and the pre-World War I hobble skirt, went out of style because the conception of woman as ornament was no longer practical or desired. As women claimed their new freedoms, they needed clothing that enabled rather than restricted them.

In the history of fashion, many of the most successful fashion designers have been those who, like Madame Vionnet, responded to or anticipated the changing times and, in particular, the changing roles of women. During World War I (1914–1918)—as would later happen during World War II—many women first went to work in weapons factories and other industries because the men who had previously held those jobs were needed on the battlefield. Women working at industrial tasks wanted clothing that was comfortable, functional, and which suited their new lifestyles and responsibilities. And women, who finally won the right to vote in 1922, also wanted clothing that expressed their new freedoms and rights as citizens. Restrictive and overly ornate clothing that implied that the wearer was, herself, merely ornamental, gave way to garments that skimmed the body, accentuating its natural lines and allowing a full range of motion. One designer, a woman from a working-class background, who anticipated women's changing needs and desires better than anyone else was the incomparable Coco Chanel.

Chanel: A Paris Original

One of the most influential designers of all time, Gabrielle "Coco" Chanel (1883–1971) started in the fashion industry as a hat designer and then turned her talents to apparel. Her winning strategy was to borrow styles, fabrics, and articles of clothing from menswear and to adapt these for women. Chanel once observed that "Fashion is architecture: it is a matter of proportions," and the proportions she favored were long and lean. (Paul Poiret dismissively referred to his rival's models as "telephone poles.") Her trademark look, in the 1920s and 1930s, was an easy-to-wear women's suit that became a wardrobe classic. Chanel had purchased a surplus stock of inexpensive knitted jersey material, used only for hosiery and underwear at that time, and she proceeded to make it into two-piece suits with a slightly gathered skirt and a long jacket. This was the first time in the history of haute couture that a "second-class" material was used as an outer garment, and Chanel's innovation of this textile revolutionized the fashion industry. Chanel also used artificial silk, developed in the 1920s, to create her famous "little black dress," a garment sometimes compared to Henry Ford's Model T because of its streamlined design, uniformity, and lack of unnecessary ornament. Her preferred palette was comprised of neutral colors such as black, beige, and white. In 1929, Chanel became one of the first haute couture designers to open a small ready-to-wear section in her *maison de couture*, a trend that caught on with other designers in the years to follow.

When France declared war on Germany in 1939, and fashion production was severely restricted, Chanel closed her salon. She decided to reopen her doors during the postwar period and mount a challenge to Christian Dior, who was making a huge splash with his "New Look." Chanel thought Dior's designs, with their tiny waists and voluminous, flowerlike skirts, were wholly unsuitable for a liberated woman. Chanel debuted her comeback collection, featuring updated versions of her classic looks, in 1953. Soon the Chanel tweed suit would become a status symbol for a whole generation of women. The beautifully constructed slim skirt and collarless jacket with patch pockets and gold buttons was just one of Chanel's designs to have inspired countless "knock-offs," or cheap imitations. However, unlike many of her fellow designers, such as Worth and Vionnet, Chanel actually encouraged such imitations, because it meant that more than just a select few wealthy clients would be able to purchase her designs. As she once said, "If a fashion is not popular with great numbers of people, it is not a fashion."

Chanel also created the first perfume to feature a designer's name: Chanel No. 5. She also designed accessories such as handbags, jewelry, and shoes, and the brand she created is one of the most recognizable and revered in the world. This fashion innovator was still working on a collection when she died in 1971 at age 87.

A Global Industry

The technical, economic, and artistic developments of the fashion world cross many cultural and national barriers, creating a living dialogue between designers—and their customers—the world over.

The American Look

The supremacy of Paris as the fashion arbiter of the world continued unchallenged until the beginning of World War II. During the German occupation of France, in June of 1940, the Nazis decided to annex the French fashion industry and relocate it to either Berlin or Vienna. Fortunately, the president of the Chambre Syndicale de la Haute Couture, couturier Lucien LeLong, secured a waiver. The Germans then placed restrictions on French fashion houses, limiting each one's collections to no more than 75 designs, approximately 25 percent of prewar production. Fabric and other materials were strictly rationed, and only very select clients—such as the wives of high-ranking Nazi party officials—wore haute couture fashions.

New York City has been the center of American fashion since the mid-nineteenth century when the development of mass production led to the growth of the apparel trades there. The seeds of the U.S. garment industry had been planted by waves of newly arriving immigrants who came to America bringing traditional skills of sewing and tailoring from their homelands. They started cottage industries in the tenements where they first settled and eventually hired workers, and formed enterprises that specialized in various aspects of manufacturing: designing and buying fabric, cutting material, and sewing. In the early twentieth century, laws were established

Fast Facts

Fashion Rations

War-time rationing of textiles in the United Kingdom led to "Utility clothes," which featured labels and buttons with a "CC41" (Civilian Clothing 1941) marking. Restrictions against wasteful cutting and use of fabric and trimmings stipulated that a dress could have no more than two pockets, five buttons, six seams in the skirt, two inverted or box pleats or four knife pleats, a maximum of 160 inches of stitching, and no superfluous decorations. London's leading fashion designers were recruited to develop a prototype Utility collection, to show that the resulting garments could still be stylish. In 1942, similar restrictions under the title of General Limitation Order l-85 were issued for the U.S. apparel industry, which remained in force until 1946.

that prevented people from manufacturing in residential structures, forcing them to move their operations into commercial loft spaces. The birth of the Fashion District, also known as the Garment Center, began in the 1920s, when a large group of garment manufacturers relocated to Seventh Avenue in Manhattan. By 1931, the one-square-mile area between Sixth and Ninth avenues and from 34th to 40th streets had the largest concentration of apparel manufacturers in the world.

Prior to the war, however, the U.S. fashion industry had always followed the dictates of French haute couture. Now, in the vacuum created by the occupying forces, American designers were isolated from French influences and began to flourish on their own terms. "The American Look" came to mean comfortable, uncomplicated garments that displayed a casual sophistication and reflected the active lifestyles of modern American women.

In 1943, the American Fashion Critics Coty Awards were established, in order to recognize the accomplishments of the domestic fashion industry. One of the most innovative and influential Americans designers of this period, and a Coty Award winner, was Claire McCardell, whose "Popover Dress"—made of denim with a wrap-around, loose silhouette and rolled-up sleeves—became the uniform of American working women during World War II. McCardell's comfortable and attractive designs, such as her "Monastic" dress and "diaper" swimsuit, earned her the distinction of appearing on the cover of *Life* magazine in 1943—one of only three designers to receive this honor.

During the war years, the American design industry, including sportswear designers, received a great deal of support from retailers such as Lord & Taylor. However, materials were rationed in the United States, as well, which influenced the shapes and styles of designs during that period.

Dior and the New Look

One designer in particular was responsible for pulling the French fashion industry out of its postwar slump and reestablishing Paris as the center of the fashion world. Christian Dior (1905–1957) joined the house of Parisian designer Lucien LeLong in 1942. When cloth rationing was lifted in 1946, Dior opened his own salon, and in the spring of 1947, he introduced his first collection. Christened the "New Look" by Carmel Snow, the editor in chief of *Harper's Bazaar*, Dior's collection became an instant success. His designs featured tiny waists, long, full skirts—an extravagance of fabric that rebuked the economies of the war years—that recalled the Belle Epoque period of the early 1900s. Dior's designs suited a political agenda, as well. Women who had worked in factories and on farms, acquiring new skills and responsibilities while men were away in combat, were now expected to relinquish those jobs and transform into domestic goddesses.

The extravagance of the "New Look" generated its share of controversy. Critics argued that the new style used too much fabric and represented a repudiation of the advances women had made during the war. Nonetheless, fashion magazines such as *Harper's* and the American edition of *Vogue* promoted Dior's designs in the United States, and in 1947 Dior received the Neiman Marcus Fashion Award, helping assure his commercial success in America. Dior's subsequent designs proved popular as well, and throughout the 1950s the House of Dior was the most successful and prestigious *maison de couture* in Paris. "Thanks to my fashion house," Dior boasted in 1956, "we celebrate the revival of French fashion."

A shrewd businessman, Dior was one of the first designers to exploit his brand-name value by granting licensing contracts. During the time that Dior dominated fashion, the business of fashion began to change from one based on studios or *ateliers* to one dominated by the global corporate conglomerates that dominate the landscape today. The fashion historian Valerie Steele makes the argument that male designers came to dominate in this changing environment because the new business models favored deep-pocketed financiers, whereas in the 1920s and 1930s a talented woman could open up a small design studio without a lot of money. As Steele writes in *The Fashion Business*, edited by Nicola White and Ian Griffiths, "As fashion was reconceived as big business and high art, rather than a small-scale luxury craft that required a minimal investment, women designers lost ground. At the turn of the century Jeanne Lanvin had opened her own business with a loan of 300 francs. [Entrepreneur] Marcel Boussac invested $500,000 in establishing the House of Dior [in 1946]". After the designer died in 1957 from choking on a fishbone, a painting of Dior and an enormous pair of shears was featured on the cover of *Time* magazine. The empire Dior built is now headed by the British designer John Galliano.

Emerging Fashion Capitals

While Dior was proud to take the credit for the resurgence of French fashion, other nations in addition to the United States were busy mounting their own challenges to that hegemony in the second half of the twentieth century.

Italian Style

Since the 12th century, Italians had enjoyed a history of success with the production of luxury textiles, shoes, and jewelry. Starting in the early twentieth century, Italy had also exported luxury items such as small leather goods. However, the Italian government had historically been too unstable to create a unified fashion center along the lines of the Parisian model. A Florentine businessman named Giovan Battista Giorgina was committed to changing that. "Count" Giorgini organized a fashion show in 1951 for an international audience and invited media representatives from high-end American department stores such as I. Magnin, Bergdorf Goodman, and Saks Fifth Avenue to review the collections on display. The U.S. representatives brought back positive reviews of the collections, and gowns by Italian designers such as Simonetta (Contessa Simonetta Visconti), Alberto Fabiani, and Roberto Capucci began to sell in the States, helping launch the Italian ready-to-wear industry.

INTERVIEW

Perspectives on Fashion's Past and Resources for Its Future

Greta Earnest
Assistant director of the library at the Fashion Institute of Technology (FIT),
New York, New York

What was your career path?

When I was in high school I was very interested in sewing and I actually think a lot girls used to—though I am not sure that they do anymore—come to fashion from that sort of personal interest. I wasn't so interested in fashion, but I was interested in making clothes and I was interested in sewing and using my hands. And I think there are still students at FIT who come to the profession that way, in a very personal relationship. So my first job was working as an hourly employee doing this specialized sewing for this woman who made custom, one-of-a-kind handbags out of fabric. She was an artist and she combined accessories and her artwork, and I was her assistant. And then I went to Paris for two years and I went to a very famous school to learn about fashion, the Chambre Syndicale de la Couture Parisienne. Then I learned that I was actually not interested in fashion in a certain way—I do not really care about the trends, but what I like is beautiful clothing and I like the relationship of clothing on people. And when I went to college I ended up studying art history. So I think I have sort of an art historical and craftsperson love of clothing rather than a fashion person love of clothing. I think the history of fashion is very interesting from a material culture/sociological kind of aspect. So my interests in fashion really lie, still, within those areas. When I got the job at FIT, it combined this previous passion I had as a teenager with a whole career of library science.

Do you have a graduate degree in library science?

Yes. In library school you can choose to emphasize different aspects of librarianship, and so since I was an art history undergraduate, I focused on specialized libraries in my library training. Before I got the FIT job, I spent [twenty years working] in architecture and design libraries. So I combined my undergraduate interests with my library science. And you can do that when you are studying library science— or you can get a dual degree in, like, art history and library science.

If you wanted to be a fashion librarian, we could certainly use some people that specialize in the field because I do not know of any with exactly that training. Most of us come from the art or the business background and then work in the fashion library field. But I do not know of anyone that has a dual master's that really specializes in fashion librarianship. I think it would be a pretty cool thing to go into because you would really have something unique to offer. And I think this is [true] internationally.

What are some of the things you enjoy most about your job?
As a librarian, having knowledge of both sides of the house, as it were, the design side and the business side, are what make the job particularly interesting, I think. That is one of the things I like about working at FIT rather than the museum world, which was very rarified, in my opinion. I really enjoy the day-to-day-ness that fashion can have. I mean, it can be elite but it also can be day to day as well.

We have specialized collections in the library that are unique to a fashion library. We have archives all oriented toward [fashion] or we get donations, people are retiring and they will give us their archives, which may include an original watercolor drawing, it may include a prospectus on starting up their new business, it may include newspaper clippings and fabric samples, idea boards. So there's that in a special collections department. In a fashion library you get to work with a lot of interesting materials and in a way memorialize important people. And the labor union in the fashion industry is very important, too. I think that previously people did not think fashion was an important area of scholarship in a certain way. But now the art history studies have changed a lot and incorporate sociology and material culture and that trend has lead to the study of material culture being thought of as a more scholarly and valid endeavor. Now there are several scholarly symposiums and conferences that acknowledge that fashion is indeed worthy of scholarly study. And if you study clothing, or the history of men's clothing, for instance, you can understand how role models in history influence clothing. For instance, it used to be that royalty were the leaders in fashion trends, and then when movies came along it became the stars rather than royalty. But if you step back and look at it not as fashion trends but through a more historical view of the role that clothing and trends play, then you start to understand the scholarly importance of things you can learn from studying fashion. It is a good time to go into that field, because graduate studies in clothing and material culture are on the rise.

(continues on next page)

INTERVIEW

Perspectives on Fashion's Past and Resources
for Its Future (continued)

How have the ways you use technology in your work evolved over time?
What I've found is that now so much is changing that the librarians now know more about some of the materials than the professionals. In the last six years there have been a lot of new resources developed, both that support business and also what we call forecasting materials. There are companies that predict what the fashion trends will be like a year from now. And that used to be all in print and now it is mostly electronic. So it is changing all the time and what's expected is that you understand and adapt to new resources as they become available from a searching perspective.

Emilio Pucci (1914–1992) was once of the first international stars of Italian fashion. Pucci popularized bright colors—hot pink, lime green, peacock blue—for the first time since World World II, and his short, clingy dresses liberated the body in a manner that was young, playful, and full of visual interest. In addition to dresses and blouses, Pucci also created scarves and tights, so that women of all income levels could own one of his creations. His name conjures up a vision of the vividly colored and patterned fabrics associated with the sixties, and many people forget that Pucci also originated the Capri pant, a huge seller during the early 1950s.

The most important Italian designer to emerge during the 1960s was Valentino. Valentino Garavani took design courses in Paris before opening his atelier in 1959 on the Via Condotti in Rome. Valentino's 1967 "White Collection" caused a sensation, as did the mid-calf hemlines he introduced in the 1970s. His impeccably cut designs manage to be both practical and luxurious, and his high-profile client list has included Jacqueline Onassis, Sophia Loren, and Gwyneth Paltrow. By the end of the twentieth century it had become increasingly difficult to run a successful couture house, however. In 1998, Valentino sold his business to the luxury conglomerate HdP.

While Italian couture was based in Rome, the industrial city of Milan, with its proximity to the textile mills of the Lake Como region, would eventually become one of the most important fashion capitals in the world because of the success of the Italian ready-to-wear industry. Menswear collections from designers all over the world are exhibited in Milan each season.

The Italians had been expertly tailoring clothes since the 14th century. One of the signatures of the modern Italian style was a kind of casual elegance, and no designer typified these traits more than Giorgio Armani. Armani is one of the few designers credited with changing the direction of men's fashion with his deconstructed jackets. He took the stiff linings out of jackets and tailored them in softer, luxurious fabrics. At the end of the seventies, Armani also created fashions for women inspired by menswear.

Italian accessories are justifiably famous with designers such as Ferragamo, "the Michelangelo of shoe designers," whose innovations in footwear brought us the cork-soled shoes, wedge heels with a concave curve, and "invisible sandals." The company has since expanded its product lines to include handbags, scarves, ties, and perfumes.

Italy continues to be a dominant force in the fashion business. Other world-famous Italian clothing designers include Versace, Moschino, Emilio Zegna, Gianfranco Ferré, Romeo Gigli, Laura Biagotti, Gucci, Roberto Cavalli, Dolce & Gabbana, and La Perla for lingerie. Missoni knits and other Italian-made textiles continue to be very much in demand, as well as leather goods from companies such as Fendi and Bottega Veneta. Miucci Prada, the most recognizable Italian designer working today, began—appropriately enough—in the accessories business, which she inherited from her grandfather.

John Stephen: The King of Carnaby Street

Judging by what one finds on the racks of today's department stores, it would seem that the human animal is one of the few species where the female is consistently more showy and elaborately colored than the male. You might be surprised to learn that throughout most of human history, men's fashions were consistently more elaborate and flamboyant than women's. This held true until about 200 years ago, when menswear adopted many of the characteristics it manifests today; typically men's clothing tends to be more conservative and somberly colored than women's, with styles that emerge and change far more slowly.

Such was the character of the prevailing sartorial landscape when a Scottish fashion radical named John Stephen (1934–2004) opened a shop in 1953 called His Clothes on London's Carnaby Street. Stephen's flamboyant designs held enormous appeal for young men who wanted to look nothing like their extremely conservative fathers. Stephen's hipster trousers, brightly colored shirts with unusual collar shapes, minikilts for men, and fitted and flared double-breasted velvet jackets were snapped up by young men eager to strut their nonconformity. Soon Stephen had fifteen different shops spread along the length of Carnaby Street. Suddenly shopping seemed liked fun, a form of recreation.

Another influential British designer who helped put London on the fashion map during this period is Mary Quant. This self-taught British designer also reacted against the conformity she saw in fashion. As Quant wrote in her autobiography, "I had always wanted young people to have a fashion of their own. To me adult appearance was very unattractive, alarming and terrifying, stilted, confined, and ugly. It was something I knew I did not want to grow into." Quant opened her Bazaar boutique in Chelsea in 1955 and began to mass-produce miniskirts. French designer André Courrèges claimed that he invented the mini and that Quant just popularized it, to which she responded that the miniskirt was invented by "the girls on the street." For the first time in fashion history, trends were bubbling up from the "bottom," from styles that young people were seen wearing on the street, instead of being dictated from the highest echelons of fashion on down. Prior to the sixties, women were far less concerned with looking young than with looking fashionable, but suddenly youth was in fashion. The schoolgirl look that Quant helped popularize was perfectly suited to the skeletal and doe-eyed model Leslie Hornby, aka Twiggy, the first supermodel.

Barbara Hulanicki opened her Biba boutique in the Kensington neighborhood of London in 1964 to sell her dusty-toned Biba makeup and clothes. The store, with its art deco décor and communal changing rooms, was a huge draw, and Hulanicki pioneered the notion of marketing a total look rather than simply selling individual pieces.

However, all youth culture was not embracing fashion. Hippie culture in the United States was actively anti-fashion, believing it was a system that supported the consumerism that they were rejecting. The hippie fashions of the 1960s took their inspiration from the past and from other countries: long skirts and blouses with ethnic embellishments for women, and fringed leather jackets and open-necked shirts for men.

In the 1971, the midwife of punk style, Vivienne Westwood, along with Malcolm McLaren, manager of the British punk band the Sex Pistols, opened a clothing shop on the King's Road in London. Punk culture was also actively anti-fashion, with its provocative focus on sex and violence, its torn and ravaged antistyle. Punk ended up having an enormous impact on Western popular culture, and its persistent influence can be seen in the work of British designers like Alexander McQueen and Zandra Rhodes and the perpetual bad boy of French fashion, Jean-Paul Gaultier.

Japanese Innovations
The first Japanese designer to achieve international recognition was Hanae Mori, who presented her collections in New York during the 1960s. Mori artfully blended Eastern and Western influences in her styles, and paved the way for other Japanese designers on the international scene such as Kenzo Takada and Kansai Yamamoto. Japanese designers who became important on the international scene during the 1980s include Issey Miyake (known for his amazing use of pleated fabrics), and Kawakubo Rei, the designing woman behind the Comme des Garçons label. Many Japanese designers have introduced radical innovations in textiles as well as avant-garde silhouettes and shapes that seem to disregard the shape of the body beneath the clothes.

The Arbiters of Style

A plethora of media outlets, from music to movies to magazines, help define the fashion sensibilities of entire demographics. The range and scope of their influence is vast, as can be seen by the following descriptions.

The Fashion Media

The dictates of fashion come from both above and below. Since the late 1960s, the latest trends have tended to bubble up from looks first seen on the street—fashions that express the mood, tastes, and interests of youth culture—and industry trend-watchers pay close attention. The fashion media also pays close attention to what hip, young people around the world are wearing on the street. Since the eighteenth century, fashion periodicals have been instrumental in communicating information about the latest styles and fashions to women eager to hear the news. As their circulation grew, periodicals

Fast Facts

Fashion Rations
Periodical Propriety

Edna Woolman Chase began working in the *Vogue* circulation department when she was 18 years old, and she became the magazine's editor in 1914—and held that position for the next 37 years. Women on Chase's staff were expected to adhere to a strict dress code: black silk stockings, white gloves, hats, and closed-toe shoes. Once a *Vogue* editor tried (unsuccessfully) to commit suicide by jumping in front of a subway train. Chase admonished her: "We at *Vogue* do not throw ourselves under subway trains, my dear. If we must, we take sleeping pills."

such as *Vogue* and *Harper's Bazaar* came to wield enormous influence in the fashion industry.

Fashion Plates

The first fashion periodicals appeared in the eighteenth century in England and France. They featured hand-colored engravings, called "fashion plates," of men and women dressed in contemporary styles of clothing. In the nineteenth century, American women—those who could afford the cost of a subscription—referred to monthly publications such as *Godey's Lady's Book, La Belle Assemblée*, and *La Gazette du Bon Ton* for information about the latest Paris fashions and other material designed to appeal to women. Eventually, fashion photography replaced the use of illustrations in these periodicals. By the turn of the twentieth century, fashion magazines such as *Harper's Bazaar* were the primary methods for spreading news of fashion trends from Paris, the capital of fashion.

The Fashion Bible

Vogue, the longest lasting, most successful, and most influential of fashion magazines, was founded by Arthur Baldwin Turnure in 1892 as a weekly publication. Condé Montrose Nast (1873–1942) began publishing the magazine in the United States in 1909, which he changed into a biweekly publication. (*Vogue* became a monthly publication in 1973.) The magazine was aimed at an elite audience and included society pages and news of charity events, country clubs, summer homes, and horseback riding, along with fashion news, book reviews, clothing patterns, and advertisements. During the Great Depression and World War II, subscriptions significantly increased. In 1932, *Vogue* became one of the first magazines to feature a color photograph on its cover. Over the years, photographers whose work has appeared in the pages of *Vogue* include Edward Steichen, Lee Miller, Cecil Beaton, Irving Penn, Richard Avedon, Helmut Newton, Annie Leibovitz, and Herb Ritts. Models who have appeared in the pages of *Vogue* have become celebrities, recognized the world over.

The list of *Vogue*'s former editors in chief reads like a Who's Who of powerful women: Josephine Redding (1892–1901), Marie Harrison (1901–1914), Edna Woolman Chase (1914–1951), Jessica Daves (1952–1963), Diana Vreeland (1963–1971), and Grace Mirabella (1971–1988). The magazine's current editor, the formidable Anna Wintour, has been at the helm since 1988. Wintour's tenure has been characterized by a renewed emphasis on journalism, a more casual cover style, and the mixing of both high and lower-priced clothing, such as the jeans paired with a Lacroix jacket featured on Wintour's inaugural cover.

"Revered for its editorial excellence and visual panache, the magazine has long functioned as a bible for anyone worshiping at the altar of luxury, celebrity, and style," wrote the critic Carolyn Weber in the *New York Times*. The fall fashion issue of the magazine is indeed known in the industry as the "fashion bible." (The 2009 film *The September Issue* goes behind the scenes to document the whirlwind of activity surrounding the production of the magazine.) When Condé Nast bought *Vogue* it had a circulation of 14,000—which had climbed to 1.2 million as of July 2009. Today, *Vogue* is published in 21 countries (the Italian edition is considered by industry pros to be the best and most beautiful fashion magazine in the world) and has spawned a menswear version, *Men's Vogue*; a version for younger readers, *Teen Vogue*; and another offspring, *Vogue Living*.

The Entertainment Industry

Though fashion periodicals such *Vogue* and *Harper's* still had their eyes trained toward Paris, American designers began establishing their reputations as sportswear designers in the 1930s. However, it was not until the fifties that distinctly American forms of dressing became popular all over the world—and remain so to this day. Early on, the entertainment industry played a key role in communicating information about fashion and style around the world. Blue jeans and the T-shirt, the most iconic and unisex of American garments, owe their popularity to the movies.

Fashion at the Movies

Movies are seen by millions of people, and over the years Hollywood has exerted a powerful influence over what people want to buy and wear. The new youth culture found its first expressions in the United States during the 1950s, where American teenagers turned to popular films for their fashion cues. Marlon Brando's appearance in the 1951 film *A Streetcar Named Desire* started a fad for wearing T-shirts, formerly considered just an undergarment. Retailers responded to the surge in customer demand and began stocking T-shirts as outerwear. Blue jeans, the single article of clothing most associated with American culture, were considered just work clothes until 1955, when James Dean wore a pair in *Rebel Without a Cause*. Suddenly, every American teenager wanted a pair of Levi's.

Costume designer Edith Head, who won eight Academy Awards for her fashions, once claimed that "A designer is only as good as the star who wears her clothes," and the movie star who had the greatest impact on fashion design was the actress Audrey Hepburn (1929–1993). Hepburn's willowy silhouette and dancer's posture, her natural style and poise, made her the perfect person to showcase the fashions of French designer Hubert de Givenchy in films such as *Funny Face* (1957) and *Breakfast at Tiffany's* (1961). No other actress before or since has had such a profound and long-lasting influence on fashion.

Diane Keaton's odd and endearing character in the 1977 Woody Allen film *Annie Hall*, whose wardrobe was designed by Ralph Lauren and styled by Keaton herself, prompted young women to copy her kooky take on menswear. During the 1980s, Madonna's punk-inspired miniskirts, torn fishnets, lacy gloves, and underwear worn as outerwear—featured in her music videos shown on MTV and the film *Desperately Seeking Susan*—inspired countless imitators. The accessories business gets a big boost from Hollywood, too. The hip look of stars Will Smith and Tommy Lee Jones in the 1997 movie *Men in Black* brought Ray-Ban sunglasses back into style again. The launch in 1994 and subsequent success of *InStyle* magazine, which focuses on celebrity fashions and trends, reflected the symbiosis between designers and movie stars at the end of the twentieth century and beginning of the twenty-first century.

Rock and Roll and Hip-Hop Style

The performances of pop stars and rock musicians have also driven fashion trends. Elvis's 1956 appearance on the *Ed Sullivan Show*, the beehive hairdos and shimmery dresses of Diana Ross and the Supremes, the Beatles' ankle boots and haircuts, Jimi Hendrix's psychedelic style, and David Bowie's androgynous space-fantasy were all seen and imitated by countless fans.

Beginning in the early 1980s, established sportswear and fashion brands such as Kangol, Nike, Adidas, and Le Coq Sportif became associated with the emerging hip-hop scene. The Tommy Hilfiger sweatshirt that Snoop Doggy Dogg wore during a 1994 appearance on *Saturday Night Live* was sold out of stores the next day. Labels such as Phat Farm, and FUBU (meaning For Us, By Us) turned hip-hop's urban street style into a multimillion-dollar business. The rapper and music producer Sean "P. Diddy" Combs, known around New York City as the "Shiny Suit Man," launched a massively successful line of sportswear in 1998 under the Sean John brand. Combs's fashion empire has since branched out to include more upscale men's suits and women's wear, once again getting a warm welcome from fashion buyers. In 2004, Combs was named CFDA Menswear Designer of the Year, beating out top designers Ralph Lauren and Michael Kors.

Categories of Fashion

Over the course of fashion history, several specific categories of fashion have emerged. Though these categories are largely defined by economics, including price points and issues of affordability, various design elements also help distinguish them from one other.

Haute Couture

Haute couture (pronounced *oat cooTOUR*) is French for "high sewing" and represents the highest expression of fashion as an art form. The first fashion designers founded the *maisons de couture* (the House of Chanel, the House of Dior) designed to cater to members of the aristocracy and the loftiest levels of the social elite, and the garments they constructed served as a visible display of wealth and a means of advertising their prominence and rightful place in the upper echelons of society. Haute couture still means the finest clothing sewed by hand to the exact measurements of the wealthiest clientele. An haute couture garment is custom-made and requires an average of three fittings with the client. An evening gown with embroidery might require several thousand hours of work. Owning such a garment might cost anywhere from $26,000 to $100,000.

To earn the distinction of an "haute couture" label, a designer must belong to the Chambre Syndicale de la Haute Couture, an organization founded in 1868 by Charles Frederick Worth and his sons to prevent couture designs from being copied. Today, members of this incredibly elite group include the design houses of Chanel, Christian Dior, Hubert de Givenchy, Christian Lacroix, Jean Paul Gaultier, and Hanae Mori, among others.

Great designers such as Dior establish design empires, or fashion houses, and then pass their unique vision on to the designers that follow in their fashionable footsteps. The current head designer at the House of Chanel, Karl Lagerfeld, must maintain the classic Chanel brand while making sure the company's designs are stylish and up-to-date.

There have been enormous changes in the fashion industry since the original *maisons de couture* opened their doors, and the very rarified type of production that they practice has fallen from fashion. The market for haute couture has been in sharp decline since the market crash of 1987 brought the excesses of the eighties to an end. Yves Saint Laurent haute couture was losing $20 million a year when it closed up operations in 2002. Only eleven fashion houses remain in Paris, supported by an ever-dwindling number of clients. While no one disputes that couture creations are an art form, they have come to play a much smaller role in the larger fashion industry, and one has to wonder whether haute couture has a future. Bergé, the former company chairman of Yves Saint Laurent, said, "Let's not kid ourselves—haute couture is finished and it is better to get out before it disappears completely."

Ready to Wear (Prêt-a-Porter)

Besides haute couture, there are two main categories of fashion design: ready to wear and mass market. The first customers of ready-to-wear clothing were men, whose wardrobes consisted of separate pieces (jackets, shirts, vests, and pants) that could be more easily mass produced than the elaborate dresses worn by women at the time. Savvy couturiers such as Chanel, recognizing the potential of ready to wear (or prêt a porter as it is called in France), began offering previously made garments in standard sizes that sported their designer labels beginning in the 1920s. Today, the designs in ready-to-wear collections are presented during Fashion Week in fashion capitals such as New York City; Milan, Italy; and Madrid, Spain. Ready-to-wear designs are produced in limited numbers from high-quality fabrics.

Mass Market

Ready-to-wear styles influence the mass market category, which consists of clothing produced quickly and cheaply, such as Gap cargo pants, for instance, or a skirt from H&M. Fashion for the masses trickles down from what shows on the runways: An exaggerated feature, such as one season's multiple layering pieces, may show up in a scaled-down version (layered T-shirts, perhaps) on the headless mannequins at Kohl's. Today's fashion industry relies more on mass market sales than it did in the past. Affordable fashions, inexpensively produced, attract a wide range of customers. Experts anticipate that the majority of job opportunities in fashion in the next decade will be in firms that design mass market clothing for sale in department stores and retail chains.

Price Range Groups for Apparel

Fashions in apparel, especially in women's wear, are currently organized in the industry according to five main price levels, although the distinctions between these levels have grown more blurred recently. The following categories are related to the more general fashion categories discussed above, but additional pricing subcategories have emerged over time.

Designer

Customers pay top prices for designer clothes, which are distinctive and original styles custom-made to a client's measurements. Each couture piece is unique and exquisitely crafted from luxurious materials, and costs thousands of dollars.

Bridgewear

The secondary lines of well-known designers have come to be known as bridgewear. These garments, produced in small quantities from fine materials, sell for many hundreds of dollars at upscale stores and dress shops. Often the apparel in bridge lines is designed by assistant designers whose work is approved by the name designer. Current examples of bridge lines include Anne Klein II, DKNY, and Calvin Klein.

Better

These garments, designed by talented experts whose names do not appear on the label, are still considered high quality, but they are more reasonably priced than bridgewear, making them accessible to more consumers. Ann Taylor and Liz Claiborne are examples of "better" apparel.

Moderate

Medium-priced merchandise with well-known brand names such as The Gap and Dockers fall into this category, which employs the most fashion designers. Aspects of these designs may be adapted from designer creations and modified to appeal to a wider range of consumers.

Budget

The lowest priced category of apparel is sold through retailers such as Old Navy, Target, and T.J. Maxx. Most of these garments are direct knockoffs of designs in more expensive price categories, which are copied by design stylists hired for that purpose. Budget apparel is manufactured inexpensively in large numbers, mostly overseas, where labor costs are lower than in the United States.

As the business changes, these pricing categories may shift or merge and new categories may be introduced. Recent developments in menswear, beginning with the introduction of the dress code known as "business casual," may force changes in pricing. For example, it can be difficult for the consumer to distinguish any significant differences between designer collections set at different price levels, such as Giorgio Armani's Emporio Armani and Armani Collezioni.

The Fashion Landscape in the New Millennium

The future of fashion is forever changing. In the new millennium customers can expect the fashion industry to cater to more of their interests and lifestyle choices beyond clothing and accessories, such as service and other convenience particulars.

Lifestyle Merchandising

Over the last two decades, department stores that specialize in fashion, such as Macy's and Bloomingdale's, have undergone a radical transformation. They have become entertainment emporiums that feature special events such as fashion shows, cocktail parties, and in-store trunk shows. In addition, instead of just offering catalogs of their wares, now some retailers send out glossy magazines to their customers, sometimes employing a full-time staff to produce them. Furthermore, whereas apparel retailers used to be simply purveyors of merchandise, now they are in the business of marketing an entire lifestyle, a style attitude, a sensibility. Ralph Lauren was the designer who pioneered this shift in merchandising. His genius was to realize that rather than trying to sell isolated items to the customer, you could market an entire way of life and persuade the customer to invest in the trappings of that lifestyle. The signature Ralph Lauren look combines classic American style with a dash of British elegance. Taking a page from the Lauren playbook, retailers such as Urban Outfitters have become curators of an ideal lifestyle for their customers. Anthropologie, a successful mass retailer that sells women's apparel and home goods with artful and interesting details, has a Web site with features that help Internet customers assemble and accessorize entire outfits and match garments to their personality types. Visual merchandisers will continue to have an important role to play in designing these evolving retail environments.

Luxury Conglomerates Replace Fashion Houses

Fashion is both an art and a business, but any student of fashion history can tell you that the business side of the industry seems to have gained the upper hand. As the famed designer Zoran once said, "You do not have to be [a] scientist to do fashion. You have to sell, and that is that." As has been true in many other industries at the end of the twentieth century, major global consolidation has radically altered the landscape of fashion. In the United States, luxury brands are still dominated by independent designers—at least for the time being. In Europe, luxury brands belong to conglomerates. Struggling *maisons du couture* along with other luxury brands have been bought up by luxury conglomerates such as Moët Hennessy Louis Vuitton (LVHM), and businessmen like Bernard Arnault are the real power brokers in fashion today. Ultimately, the most successful people in the field seems to be those who have instinctively understood that the fashion industry is fueled not by need (nobody "needs" a $2,000 handbag) but by desire. As Ralph Lauren once said, "I do not design clothes, I design dreams."

A Brief Chronology

1764: James Hargreaves invents the spinning jenny, the first machine to improve upon the spinning wheel. He patents it in 1770.

1792: Eli Whitney invents the cotton gin.

1804: Joseph Marie Jacquard invents the Jacquard loom.

1824: La Jardinière Maison department store opens in Paris.

1830: *Godey's Lady's Book* launches in the United States.

1846: Elias Howe patents the sewing machine.

1850: Synthetic polymers developed.

Mid-1850s: Amelia Bloomer promotes costume of Turkish trousers under a skirt, later known as bloomers, to give women more freedom of movement.

1858: Charles Worth establishes the first fashion house in Paris; R.H. Macy & Co. opens as a dry goods store in New York City.

1872: Levi Strauss patents his hard-wearing pants, the prototype for blue jeans.

1892: *Vogue* magazine launched.

1900: International Ladies Garment Workers Union (ILGWU) formed.

1902: Macy's department store moves to Herald Square in New York.

1909: The Uprising of the Twenty Thousand, a general strike in the garment industry to protest wage cuts and poor working conditions.

1911: The Triangle Shirtwaist Factory fire.

1913: Gabrielle "Coco" Chanel opens first boutique in Deauville, France.

1914: First brassiere patented.

1914–1918: World War I. Women begin wearing pants, military uniforms influence civilian clothing.

1922: Women get the vote.

1923: Zipper patented.

1926: The little black dress designed by Coco Chanel makes its debut.

1929: New York stock market crash; beginning of the worldwide Great Depression.

1930: First instance of a designer logo to appear on a garment: French tennis star Rene Lacoste, known as "the Crocodile," manufactures a tennis shirt with an embroidered crocodile.

1940–1945: World War II forces many Paris couture houses to close.

1942: Claire McCardell's "Popover" dress.

1947: Christian Dior's "New Look" reestablishes Paris as the capital of fashion, revives the haute couture industry.

1955: Mary Quant opens her boutique Bazaar in London's Chelsea neighborhood, introduces shortest skirt in the history of fashion, the "mini."

1956: Balenciaga's "sack" dress.

Early 1960s: Pierre Cardin becomes the first designer to license his name for various products. He creates the first ready-to-wear lines.

Mid-1960s: London established as a fashion center.

1964: Biba boutique opens in London.

1966: Yves Saint Laurent introduces the trouser suit for women.

1976: Diane von Furstenberg creates her best-selling jersey wrap dress.

1978: Kenzo's "Egyptian" collection.

1981: MTV debuts; Rei Kawakubo shows her fashions in Paris.

1984: Donna Karan launches line.

1987: U.S. stock market crash.

1990s: Alexander McQueen, Stella McCartney.

1993: Issey Miyake's Pleats Please line.

2008: Stock market crash; beginning of global recession; Yves Saint Laurent dies at age 71.

Chapter 2

State of the Industry

The fashion industry, familiarly called "the rag trade," is a multi-billion-dollar global business that employs about 4.7 million people in the United States alone. While the title of fashion designer is the most high profile of jobs in this industry, a position usually associated with wealth and glamour, just a small percentage of people working in fashion have this title embossed on their very chic (and beautifully designed) business cards. Most jobs in the fashion industry fall into three general categories:

→ **Fashion design production**, which includes jobs such as fashion and accessory designer, fashion merchandiser, product manager, clothing pattern maker, pattern grader, and textile machine operator.

→ **Fashion marketing and merchandising**, which includes jobs such as fashion buyer, fashion coordinator, retail merchandiser, visual merchandiser, retail store manager, and boutique owner.

→ **Fashion media and promotions**, which includes jobs such as fashion stylist, fashion writer, graphic designer, fashion editor, PR specialist, and fashion photographer.

Other positions in the fashion industry include model, costume designer for film, television, and theater productions, and personal stylist.

People employed in the fashion design production side of the industry create sketches or models (by hand or on the computer) of original garments, shoes, handbags, and other fashion accessories. They usually specialize in a particular area of apparel design, such as women's, men's, or children's clothing, lingerie, or sportswear. A *fashion designer* might be responsible for every aspect of the design and marketing process, or she or he might be part of a team that includes *pattern makers*, who translate a designer's sketch into a finished garment, *production managers*, who oversee the production of a line of apparel, and *fashion merchandisers*, whose job it is to introduce and promote those designs in the marketplace.

Professionals who work in fashion marketing and merchandising create and identify trends and market the products created by fashion designers. They design advertising campaigns to promote clothing lines or accessories. Fashion merchandisers may be employed in retail or wholesale sales.

Editors and *writers* employed in fashion media and promotions may contribute to industry newspapers, magazines, or trade journals, or they may be employed in new media and be responsible for bringing the latest news about styles and trends to fashion blogs and Web sites. *Fashion photographers, illustrators,* and *graphic designers* are employed by catalogs and magazines both in print and online.

Fashion and the Economy

As a massive, multibillion-dollar global industry, the fashion business mirrors the larger economy and vice versa. This industry has a profound influence on the world markets and, in turn, is influenced by the ups and downs of those markets.

The relationship between fashion and the economy is further complicated by the fact that articles of clothing and fashion accessories are not simply commodities—products that are bought and sold and consumed, like toothpaste or breakfast cereal. What we choose to wear constitutes a complex form of social communication, a continually evolving visual language, and fashion embodies this language. Changes in the global economy are reflected not only in whether a certain company opens X number of new stores in different cities, or hires or lays off X number of workers, but in the fashions themselves—from the amounts and types of fabrics used and the kinds of silhouettes and embellishments, to the color palettes in the collections that designers present each season. A Wall Street theory called the "hemline effect" actually claims that the length of women's hemlines can serve as a reliable indicator of the state of the economy: If the market is down and stock prices drop, so do women's hemlines. When the market rallies, shorter skirts come back into fashion. Some financial analysts swear by the hemline effect. Whether or not you subscribe to that particular theory, it is indisputable that fashion and the business of fashion go hand in glove.

The most recent example of the fascinatingly complex relationship between fashion and finance is the 2008–2009 economic recession and the profound impact it had on this global industry. The first decade of the new millennium ended with gloomy economic forecasts and distressing reports of companywide layoffs.

As was the case with previous economic downturns, such as the recession of 1981–1982, and the one that followed the stock market crash of October 1987, the fashion industry had a rough ride in 2008. Retailers cut more than 500,000 jobs, which amounted to 20 percent of the 2.6 million layoffs that occurred in the United States overall. New York Fashion Week saw a reduced number of shows at Bryant Park, and nearly 10 percent of the workforce at Chanel received pink slips that year (the famed design house's worst layoff since Coco Chanel fired all her staff at the beginning of World War II).

Another sign of the times was an increased focus on affordable and cheaply produced styles for the mass-market consumer. Today, much of the labor on these inexpensive mass-market items is outsourced—the work is completed overseas or in other countries where labor is much cheaper than in the United States—and the loss of these manufacturing jobs has inevitably impacted the American job market. In 1980, the U.S. apparel industry employed over one million workers; as of 2006 it employed only one-third of that amount. As of 2009, that number has likely decreased even further.

Fashion, as you no doubt have already discovered, is a perpetually competitive business. During periods of economic stress, the industry becomes even more competitive, and anyone seeking to rise in the rag trade has to find new and inventive ways of distinguishing him- or herself as the best candidate in a crowded field.

Consider it a creative challenge. If you are already employed in the fashion business, it is more than likely that you are a highly creative and innovative person. Many of the same abilities that got you a job in the first place can be put to good use as you strive to climb the career ladder. Recent changes in the industry have created

Keeping
in Touch

Industry Contacts

In an uncertain economy it is especially important that you keep in touch with people in the profession—not just people in the same position as you but with photographers, magazine editors, stylists, textile professionals, and anyone else associated with the industry. Calling someone to commiserate about a recent layoff might lead to some useful information. If you have been given the pink slip, it is a good time to send out an e-mail letting everyone know you are looking for work and that any contacts or suggestions would be welcomed. Contact people frequently—stay on their radar—but keep it brief. Patricia Nugent, a small-business owner who manages an archive of antique textiles, says she makes sure she calls at least five clients a day, to find out how their businesses are going and just to keep in touch. When the economy improves, people will remember your efforts and may be in a position to help you.

unforeseen opportunities, and that is where you should be concentrating your attention.

A declining market for luxury items means that jobs in high-end fashion may become increasingly rare, but it also has resulted in a resurgence of consumer interest in affordable and stylish mass-market apparel or a willingness on the part of buyers to invest in well-made basics that will last for several seasons. Anticipating this trend, savvy designers such as Isaac Mizrahi, Marc Jacobs, and Vera Wang have successfully tapped into this market by creating *diffusion lines*—lower-priced, mass-market versions of their more expensive labels. Retailers of so-called fast fashion, such as the Swedish retailer H&M, California's Forever 21, and the U.K.'s Topshop, which opened a 25,000-foot, four-story retail space in New York's SoHo in April 2009, were also launching new stores and hiring in a frugal economy. The bargain retailer Dollar General announced plans to add as many as 4,000 jobs in 2009 and to open 450 stores in many areas of the country hard-hit by the recession.

At the beginning of 2009, there were more glimmers of hope. According to the U.S. Commerce Department, in January 2009 retailers reported a 1 percent increase in sales (to $344.6 billion) from the month before. While this might not seem like much, it represented the biggest increase since November 2007 and thus was taken as a heartening sign by many. The fact that Americans spend $82 billion on clothing each year means there will be opportunities in the world of fashion available to those who keep informed about new trends and developments in the industry. As of this writing, individuals with skills and experience in production, technical design, computer-aided design (CAD), graphics, visual/merchandising, and retail/wholesale sales are still in demand.

Statistics on Employment, Wages, and Profits

Knowing basic employment trends as well as details on the discrepancies in wages and salaries throughout the fashion industry can help tremendously when seeking employment.

Fashion Design

According to the Bureau of Labor Statistics, fashion designers in the United States held about 20,000 jobs in 2006. The majority of these jobs were concentrated in the industry centers of New York City and Los Angeles. About 28 percent of fashion designers worked for apparel, piece goods (fabrics made and sold in standard lengths, also called yard goods), and notion merchant wholesalers, and the remainder worked for corporate offices involved in the management of companies, clothing stores, performing arts companies, and specialized design services.

Forecasts for employment in the industry anticipate that the employment of fashion designers in cut-and-sew manufacturing (clothing made from fabric produced in other establishments) will not decline as fast as other industries because firms will likely keep the design work in-house.

Earnings in fashion design can be difficult to summarize, since they vary widely, depending on the employer and the years of experience an individual has in the field. Starting salaries for fashion designers have tended to be very low until employees have established themselves in the industry. Median annual earnings for fashion designers were $62,610 as of May 2006—with the lowest 10 percent earning less than $30,000 per year. On the other hand, top-drawer fashion designers, those in the top 10 percent, can earn as much as $170,120 annually.

According to the Bureau of Labor Statistics, almost one-quarter of all fashion designers are self-employed. Freelance designers who have a client base and a large network to draw upon have a greater chance of success than those who do not, and it also helps to be extremely organized, well disciplined, and to have a good head for business when you are working in your own. Those in the know will caution: Do not believe the myth that freelancers make so much more than salaried workers; remember, they have to pay for their health care out of pocket, and they do not earn anything when they take a vacation.

Despite the fact that 25 percent of all fashion designers work on a freelance basis, new freelance jobs in fashion have become rare, and competition for those jobs is fierce. While one might assume that a company forced to lay off full- or part-time workers would turn to freelancers to help pick up the slack, some firms have instead opted to freeze hiring and ask the people on staff to shoulder more of the work. Those companies that are hiring may offer lower salaries with higher workloads.

Those who can make the most of the job market will be employees able to showcase a wide range of skills and who are highly versatile and willing and able to respond without complaint to an employer's changing needs. Show your manager or boss that you are flexible—which can mean demonstrating your willingness to relocate, to accept less money (painful as that may be), or to cheerfully assume responsibilities that you did not originally sign on to do—that is, you need to look for opportunities to show that you are a "team player." In other words, divas need not apply. If you can do this, when the economy improves, you will be in a far better position to negotiate with your employer when the opportunity arises.

Production and Technical Design Positions

As of March 2009, robust sales of more affordable fashion and of outerwear have meant that firms were hiring workers in the moderately priced, mass-market, and outerwear categories. Jobs in production and technical design, as well as in sales, have proven far more numerous than those in apparel design.

Workers in fashion production have a very hands-on role in the industry: They may be employed as *pattern makers, hand sewers,* or operate sewing machines; they also may work in *textile manufacturing*. Annual salaries for these types of production jobs can range from $20,000 to $50,000, though highly skilled pattern makers may earn as much as $150,000. The number of people entering the pattern making trade has declined, so experienced pattern makers are in demand. *Production managers* oversee all the manufacturing processes in the fashion industry, including quality control. This is a fairly senior position, so salaries range from $45,000 to $90,000. The position of *technical designer* has emerged in the last few decades as a result of offshore manufacturers making a broader range of products; among other tasks, the technical designer provides specifications and information about constructing garments to offshore customers (in Sri Lanka, for example), so he or she needs a strong background in pattern making. Salaries for technical designers vary, with salaries in New York City posting 29 percent higher than nationwide averages. Average salaries for technical designers in different U.S. cities are: New York City, $72,000; Houston, $54,000; Los Angeles, $54,000; and Minneapolis, $49,000.

The retail industry accounts for 11.6 percent of all employment in the United States. The largest employers of retail salespersons are department stores, apparel stores, and clothing and accessories stores. U.S. fashion retailers who opened new stores in 2009 include Aeropostale, American Eagle, Urban Outfitters, Gap, American Apparel, and Abercrombie & Fitch, showing that apparel sales in the youth market continued to be strong, despite a general trend toward downsizing. Turnover of sales positions in the industry has almost always been high, in part because wages for these types of positions tend to be fairly low: The annual mean salary in retail apparel sales is $20,550, under $10 an hour. In addition, retail salespersons often end up working 10- to 12-hour days, as well as on weekends and holidays. But high turnover means there will always be jobs somewhere, and these positions can lead to more lucrative positions in retail management, marketing, and the growing field of information technology (IT) in retail, where annual salaries can range from $40,000 to $110,000.

Green Jobs

In response to the growing demand in the United States and overseas for sustainable fashion, which strives to minimize its negative impact on the environment and the planet's limited resources, there are an increasing number of jobs in eco-friendly design for packaging and accessory brands, as well as positions for eco-consultants. (For more about eco-consciousness is the fashion industry, see below, "Clothing for a Small Planet.") Eco-consultants often work on a freelance basis or for small companies with fewer than 20 employees.

Current Trends

In addition to the economy, four of the biggest trends influencing the fashion business are (1) new technologies, (2) new media, (3) the greening of the fashion industry, and (4) labor practices and fair trade issues. The latest software programs have changed the way designers work and have accelerated all stages of the design process. Consumers discuss and read about styles and trends on blogs or social networking sites, and unknown designers can potentially reach millions of potential customers via the Internet. The fashion industry is in the midst of a radical makeover: For much of its history, the industry has relied upon the systematic exploitation of countless numbers of low-paid or unpaid laborers and the unchecked exploitation of the planet's natural resources.

Fast Facts

Luxury Spending

Economic woes do not always equal reduced luxury spending. As was recently the case in Australia, the devalued Australian dollar meant that tourists were suddenly buying up high-end items such as classic Chanel handbags—with the result that some of Melbourne's luxury boutiques reported 300 percent higher sales.

Today, fashion designers and consumers are increasingly aware of the human and environmental toll that the industry has taken. A global effort is currently underway to change the way fashion does business. Insiders will tell you that, for all these reasons, this is a challenging and fascinating time to be working in this creative and rapidly evolving industry.

New Technologies

Several technological developments have helped streamline the fashion industry in recent years, making it more efficient for both designers and customers alike.

CAD and CAM

It would be difficult to think of a profession that has not been profoundly changed by the advent of information technologies, and the fashion industry is no exception. Some of the most important of these new technologies are computer-aided design, or CAD, and computer-aided manufacturing, or CAM.

Fashion houses began using CAD programs, versions of which were first employed by architects and engineers, during the 1990s in order to reduce waste and costs, and to speed up production. Continuing refinements in artificial intelligence and animation make it possible for a designer to adjust fit on a virtual model, and view designs in various shapes and colors, saving the time and money of creating actual garment samples. Two leading producers of this type of software include Gerber Technology, a firm that creates software packages used by the Gap, Levi's, and Abercrombie & Fitch, among other companies, and the French company Lectra, whose clients include Dolce & Gabbana, Christian Dior, Eddie Bauer, and Calvin Klein. Firms such as these offer modular software packages designed to meet specific industry needs, including programs for design, 3D prototyping, size grading, pattern making, and integration with automated textile-cutting machines. Some examples of CAD programs include software such as StyleDraper Pro, which enables designers to apply virtually any fabric to a live model, thus creating an infinite range of samples, and ColorVision, which allows the user to recolor any scanned fabric or image.

CAD programs such as these have revolutionized the textile industry. They are easy to operate and save both the time and expense of design labor. They allow the designer to work from anywhere, creating data that can be easily stored and transmitted. Digital swatches can be stored without the need for physical inventory space, and designs can be easily customized—corrections and editing can be accomplished without delays or cost increases.

Many CAD/CAM programs are tailor-made for fashion's global economy. For instance, the artificial intelligence in pattern-making software requires that only measurements be input; it is not necessary to include information about garment construction, which would need to be translated into the native tongue of a foreign factory worker. This enables a design to be manufactured anywhere in the world.

Today, nearly every design school offers instruction in CAD/CAM programs. While CAD programs have not yet replaced traditional skills such as hand-sketching, pattern-making, and draping, anyone wishing to further their career in fashion design production today will be expected to have some degree of familiarity with these programs. The candidate who combines a solid basis of fashion fundamentals with a working knowledge of the latest technologies in the field will have the best shot at the position.

The Rise of Online Retailing

The Internet represents an almost unlimited resource for fashion marketers and retailers. Images and information appearing online can instantly reach millions of consumers all over the world. The Internet has become a billion-dollar business opportunity for the fashion industry. According to Nielsen Net Ratings, slightly more American women than men use the Internet (51 percent), and much of that time online is spent shopping. Net-a-Porter.com—a "premier online luxury fashion retailer"—maintains a Web site that is viewed by over 1.8 million women each month. Online fashion retailers such as Bluefly.com and Zappos.com for footwear and other kinds of apparel have performed very well, weathering the ups and downs of the market, and Zappos was featured on the cover of *Fortune* magazine's "100 Best Companies to Work For" issue of 2009.

Some of the hottest sites are interactive, encouraging feedback from consumers, such as Threadless and Collarfree, community-based T-shirt companies that seek online graphic design submissions and reproduce the most popular designs, which are then sold via the Web site. The online fashion company Us Trendy (Ustrendy.com) combines the design competition concept of sites like Threadless and throws budding fashion designers and models into the mix. Aspiring designers can upload their portfolios to the site. Then visitors to the site vote on the designs they like, and Us Trendy produces and sells the most popular designs in their online store. Models can also upload their best shots for users to vote on—the highest rated models work the catwalk at Us Trendy fashion shows.

E-commerce has not just been a boon for big companies, either. The Internet affords opportunities for smaller retailers to advertise and sell their designs without the expense of renting a storefront. Kamie Chang Kahlo, a Seattle-based designer who created the Internet site Adelitastyle (Adelitastyle.com), opted to sell her clothing designs and those of other local designers entirely online when local rents became too high for her business to sustain. Popular Web sites such as Etsy.com that specialize in handmade goods (anything from clothing to accessories to stationary and art), enable any aspiring designer to open a virtual store and to advertise and sell her or his wares online.

New Media

We live in an accelerating culture of fast food and fast fashion, where communications occur in real time and at lightning speed on social network sites such as Twitter and Facebook. In a trend-based industry dedicated to delivering the latest styles to the selling floor as quickly possible, new types of media such as fashion blogs, magalogue-style Web sites, as well as online newspapers and magazines have become enormously popular and influential; they have also created new sources of employment in the industry.

Fashion Blogs

Short for *Weblogs*, blogs have become one of the favorite ways for retailers to quickly generate lots of up-to-the-minute content for their Web sites. Fashion blogs offer readers a source for the latest information about styles and trends and encourage them to check

Everyone
Knows

Crunching the Numbers

People in the rag trade will tell you that online salary calculators are unrealistic and inaccurate for the fashion industry, especially in New York City, where many of the jobs are concentrated. Bear in mind, too, that the average rent for a one-bedroom apartment in Manhattan is a staggering $2,500 per month. Unless you have a hefty nest egg to draw upon, that is going to eat up a sizeable portion of your monthly earnings. So if you are negotiating for a starting salary or an increase in your current pay, be sure you talk to some people in comparable positions in the same city where you hope to work—and, even better, the company where you plan to apply—before you undersell yourself or take yourself out of the running by quoting a number that is way out of the ballpark.

in repeatedly—and repeated visits by users increase the sites' search engine rankings. Blogs are an ideal way for online retailers to direct consumers to their Web sites, and they need to hire bloggers to generate all this Web content. A related job, called "blog-scraping," a type of social Web analysis, involves monitoring different blogs—essentially listening in on the conversations that consumers have with one another—to detect emerging trends in the fashion industry.

Magalogues

This rather clunky term for a Web site that is part magazine, part catalog has recently gained currency. The best magalogue-style Web sites, such as the one maintained by the British online retailer Asos. com, are easy to navigate and contain news, trend alerts, and the very latest "hot buy" items. Such Web sites have become increasingly important marketing devices for fashion retailers, who depend on a growing number of technical and non-technical staff members to keep them up and running and chock full of compelling content.

The Internet has generated a world of new opportunities for job seekers in the fashion industry, and not just because it makes it much easier to search for jobs or to post a résumé for employers to find. A whole gamut of Internet-related jobs, such as Web developer, Web marketing specialist, Web design business analyst, and director of online marketing, are available to individuals with the right technical backgrounds. The salary range for a typical position in the U.S. Web industry is $55,000 to $74,000.

Clothing for a Small Planet

There's no question about it: The fashion industry has historically been extremely tough on the planet. Beginning in the late 1980s, "green" was suddenly very much in fashion again. Ecological themes and motifs started showing up on the runways, and designers began working with eco-friendly fabrics such as organic cotton, hemp, jute, and bamboo. Apparel companies such as Ellen Tracy and Esprit promoted environmental causes through their advertising as well as through their well-advertised contributions to these causes. Glossy fashion rags, such as *Vanity Fair, Marie Claire, Elle,* and *Mademoiselle* each rushed to put out a "green issue," though regrettably few of these magazines were printed on recycled paper or used soy-based inks in the printing process.

The irony of fashion embracing environmental awareness was not lost on many observers: The industry depends, after all, upon premeditated obsolescence and waste—styles come and out of fashion, and once they are out they become disposable. However, this business is also driven by consumers, and consumers were suddenly demanding clothing that was fashion forward and eco-friendly, both easy on the eyes and easy on the planet.

Despite fears that concerns about the foundering economy would overshadow worries about the state of the environment, consumer demand for green fashion has persisted. Today, top designers like Stella McCartney and Linda Loudermilk (the so-called "Vivienne Westwood of eco") have turned their commitments to earth-friendly fashion into highly successful businesses. It does not hurt to have A-list celebrities such as Leonardo diCaprio and Robert Downey, Jr., modeling your designs on the covers of glossy magazines, either, as was the case with Loudermilk. Actress Pamela Anderson has even teamed up with the couturier Richie Rich to launch a line of eco-friendly designs, due to debut in the summer of 2009.

There has been a backlash against the wastefulness of so-called "fast fashion," as well. In August 2008, the House of Lords (the upper house of the British parliament) issued a report singling out the apparel retailer Topshop, criticizing the popular store and other retailers for creating throwaway fashion that winds up in landfills when the next hot style comes along. Magazines entirely devoted to green fashion have debuted, such as *Boho*, the online magazine *Coco Eco* (whose slogan is "Good Green Glam!"), and *Lü*.

Today, the new environmentalism (unlike the old, 1970s environmentalism) has permeated almost all aspects of the fashion business and will undoubtedly give rise to a new range of related eco-jobs.

The green movement has also spurred innovations in textile development. Polar fleece made from fiber spun out of plastic bottles has been on the scene since 1981; more recently, eco-friendly materials such as Modal (made with reconstituted cellulose from beech trees) and soy and fiber yarn (known as "vegetable cashmere") have appeared. (A new kind of silk has also been spun from milk fibers, but its eco-friendliness has been fiercely contested on green fashion blogs.) According to the EPA, in 2007 nearly 12 million tons of textile waste was created from pre- and post-consumer waste. The Martex Fiber Southern Corp. textile company reuses the "cut and sew" waste that winds up on its cutting room floors, including seam waste from T-shirt manufacturing and toe clippings from the sock-making process, by "refiberizing" it into fluff, which can then be spun into new yarn. Enough companies have adopted such cost-saving (and Earth-saving) practices that cut and sew waste has become harder to come by.

The recycling aesthetic has pervaded fashion in the forms of garments constructed from recycled fabrics (T-shirts made from recycled yarn, for instance) and reworked vintage pieces. Initially found just in vintage and green-leaning boutiques, reworked, limited edition pieces by labels such as Renewal have been showing up on the racks of major retailer chains such as Urban Outfitters.

While green fabrics can be costly, consumer demand has prompted textile manufacturers everywhere to begin producing more eco-friendly materials. At the biannual Texworld textile trade fair in Paris in February 2009, 60 of the 660 firms from around the world showcased an investment in "green" textiles in their exhibits. According to Texworld organizers, that number represents a considerable increase from previous fairs. "Eco-friendly is our key item; the market has changed," said a manager at the South Korean textile firm Ludia, which exhibited at Texworld. Top textile producers such as China, India, and Bangladesh, often criticized for being big industrial polluters, are listening as well, and have been begun producing more eco-friendly textiles. Regulation is strict, however, and earning the right to label a textile as organic or eco-friendly remains both complicated and costly for the manufacturer. "China is receiving increasing orders for eco-friendly textiles, with European customers handing you a thick book like a dictionary with standards and certifications, from the raw material to the finished product," says Yan York, the Chinese representative for Texworld.

Today, eco-consciousness is so integrated into the fashion industry that some argue that green has become mainstream. As evidence, they point to the recent decision by the publishers of *Vanity Fair* to discontinue publication of its annual "green issue" in 2009. Nonetheless, it is worth hazarding a guess that issues with unsustainable business practices and industrial pollution will continue to be an important source of new jobs in the future, and particularly during periods of economic recovery.

Ethical Fashion

Closely related to the green movement in the fashion industry is the growing consumer demand for "ethical fashion"—fashion that incorporates ethical practices such as the conservation of resources and protection of the environment, fair trade and fair wages, and the assurance of healthy and safe working conditions for those who labor in the industry. Fairtrade Labeling Organizations International (FLO), an umbrella group of 20 certifying groups formed in 1997, is part of a worldwide network of Fair Trade organizations. The goals of these organizations are to (1) work with marginalized producers and workers to help them achieve greater economic security and self-sufficiency, (2) to empower producers and workers as stakeholders in their own organizations, and (3) to actively promote greater equity in international trade.

In a survey of fifteen countries commissioned by the FLO, three-quarters of the shoppers agreed that apparel companies should "actively support community development in developing countries." The survey also found that 57 percent of Americans would be willing to spend at least five percent more for Fair Trade Certified products, with nine out of ten respondents trusting the labels of the Fairtrade Certification Mark and the North American Fair Trade Certified trademark. These labels guarantee that various economic, social, and environmental criteria have been met in the production and trade of a product.

Originally, socially conscious fashion had a reputation for being overpriced and unfashionable. This trend is quickly shedding that reputation as ethical fashion becomes more sophisticated and fashion forward. The ethical fashion movement has spawned dedicated events, such as the Ethical Fashion Show, the world's largest event devoted to fair-trade fashion and sustainable style. Since its creation in 2004, the event, which opens annually in a succession of cities, has showcased both new and established designers and helped raise industry awareness about conditions of workers in the apparel business.

While the ethical fashion movement has been most visible in the United Kingdom and in Europe, it has been gaining momentum in the United States. Some retailers, such as American Apparel, have based their success in part on their commitment to selling clothing that is proudly labeled "sweatshop free." In late 2008, American Apparel held biweekly open calls for jobs in New York City. Compared to November of the previous year, sales of the youth-oriented clothing store increased by 6 percent. In fact, social consciousness sells: Apparel companies that have proved themselves leaders in bringing about enlightened environmental and social policies have a history of outperforming their competitors. FLO-CERT, an organization that inspects and certifies producer groups in more than 70 countries across Europe, Asia, Africa, and Latin America, employs workers with backgrounds in economic and environmental studies and manufacturing as well as with labor and legal experience.

Possible Future Trends

The fashion industry continues to grow as designers respond to changing economic and technological developments as well as aesthetic sensibilities.

KO-ing the Knockoffs
Knockoffs, the counterfeit currency of the fashion business, are a huge problem in the industry. These cheap imitations of luxury goods, sporting fake logos (fake Louis Vuitton handbags and imitation Prada sunglasses, for instance), are hawked with impunity on every street corner in Manhattan. U.S. Customs and Border Protection seized $272.7 million in counterfeit and pirated goods in 2008—38 percent increase from 2007. (You might be surprised to learn that Coco Chanel, whose designs have inspired countless knockoffs, actually encouraged imitations. "I want my dresses to go out on the street," the designer once declared.) The Design Piracy Prohibition Act is a bill (S. 1957) pending in the U.S. Senate that would treat designs as a creative project, like original works of art, as opposed to clothing which is considered a "useful article" and not eligible for copyright protection under current laws related to apparel. This bill would amend the Copyright Act to include a three-year term of protection for fashion designs. It would also create a searchable database of designs that have filed for protection. If this bill eventually becomes law, it could generate many jobs specializing in fashion law and design copyright enforcement.

Curves on the Runway
The days of the über-skinny, size zero fashion model may be numbered. In 2006, after the ultra-thin Uruguayan model Luisel Ramos died of heart failure after stepping off the runway, organizers of Madrid Fashion Week began barring models who were too thin (anyone with a body mass index, or BMI, of less than 18) from the catwalk. Later that year, Italian fashion designers banned size zero models from the runways. Fuller figured models, and older models, too, have been appearing in fashion shows, heralding a shift toward

INTERVIEW

Opportunities in the Industry

Patricia Nugent
Director, Patricia Nugent Design and Textiles, Seattle, Washington

How would you describe what you do?

I sell antique textiles and vintage textiles to designers and to companies so that they can use them as inspiration or concepts for new products. So I may have a pattern from 1860, and someone may buy that pattern and reinterpret it to print on home textiles or a T-shirt, or wall coverings, or whatever. Someone might buy a silk ribbon from me that is circa 1820 and they might print it on a piece of cotton to use on a trim on a little girl's T-shirt.

How did you get started in this business?

I purchased two archives from a woman who had built an archive—it was very American in sensibility—and then I purchased a second archive from a French woman who had built a French and Italian archive, and she bought her textile pieces and swatches in Paris and Lyon and London over the last forty years.

How would you describe your career path in the fashion business? How did you arrive at the place you are now?

My background is in clothing and textile design. I have a four-year degree, a bachelor of arts degree from the University of Washington, and I did a fifth year of design study at the fashion school of the city of Vienna in Austria, and my first job after my fifth year was as an assistant designer in a skiwear company in Seattle. And people told me I needed to move to New York if I wanted to be a designer, but I was very fortunate and I did not have to do that. After skiwear design I did sweater design and then I opened my own design and merchandising business.

What were some of your responsibilities?

I worked on the trend and concept with the senior designer. I developed the looks, I helped develop the fabrics, the color stories, did the actual sketching, the designing, and did the actual specification sheets so that the patterns could be made and the garment could be sampled the first time—and then after first sample stage we would prove out production—that would be grading and developing the sizes that you would offer a garment in, and then get the garment into production so that you would have enough goods to deliver to your customers.

Meanwhile, of course, in a company the salesmen are selling and production is producing and so on. It is a huge team effort in the apparel business. So after skiwear and outwear for brands and my own independent business, I was hired at Cutter & Buck as vice president of production, and then I moved from vice president of production into vice president of merchandising and design, where I did the merchandising, the line planning, the pricing, managed the design process, the designers themselves. I had a very talented group of people—I was very, very lucky. We took the company public and went through that process, so along with my fashion background and my art background I also had a business background. My minor in school was business, so that I could combine fashion and apparel with business. The beauty of that is it allowed me to be a merchandiser. It allowed me to understand pricing, profit margins, importing, all of the financial processes that go with manufacturing domestically and importing. And then after Cutter & Buck I worked with Ex Officio for about a year. Then I decided to buy one of these archives, and I actually bought the whole business. I bought the customer base and the customer list and so on. That is what I've been doing since 2005.

Are you a specialist in textile trends?

One of things I provide my [customers] is I only show them what is important from a fashion standpoint in any given season. For example, right now we're having a very big resurgence of California surf and beach looks from the 1940s and 1950s. That is a trend. So, I am a trend specialist in that sense. It is a niche business. Right now I think there are about 10 of us in the country who do it. There are also people who sell original patterns, surface design, designed by artists, and they are artists' representatives. They sell print and pattern that is [created] by surface designers and textile designers, and it is a very interesting field, and there's many, many of those around in America, and also England and France and Italy.

Who are your clients?

I have customers who make products in the kids' business, the women's business, the mens' business, and the home business, and also paper goods. I sell Staples patterns to use on their printed and patterned file folders. Some people who are related to my business license the patterns they have, so, for example, they may license a pattern to a company like Staples or Hallmark or Target, and they get a royalty on every piece of the pattern that is sold by the company who licenses it. [Other clients I've had are] Gap, Abercrombie [& Fitch], Ann Taylor, American Eagle, Old Navy, Banana Republic, and some of the higher

(continues on next page)

INTERVIEW

Opportunities in the Industry (continued)

end people like Ralph Lauren. Also smaller, independent designers who have small independent lines, like Bedhead Pajamas and so on, locally in Seattle, Eddie Bauer and Tommy Bahama.

What do you enjoy most about your job?
The side of this business that is most interesting to me is working with designers. Something that people might want to know about going into design is if they do not feel that they are really good textile designers but they are apparel designers or they are production specialists or something like that, they can work with people like myself and my competitors to develop their lines because we generally have background in line development. So we can help them be really good at what they do by giving them a collection of patterns that are already coordinated and that work together and are trend-right. We can help designers do a better job in their planning.
I had a professor at the University of Washington who said to me, "Pat, one of the most enjoyable things in life is to be so good at something that the world comes to your door for your knowledge, so that you do not have to go to the world's door." And that always stuck with me. All of my competitors are very knowledgeable about textiles, about history, about methods of printing and design. A certain amount of why my customers come to me is for my knowledge.

Are mentors important in this career?
I think they are very important, and learning from someone can mean following in their footsteps or not following in their footsteps. I think we all tend to seek out people like that, and it is a good thing. People

more realistic bodies in the modeling profession. If you are an aspiring model, this is good news for your health.

CAD Backlash?
Many have embraced the latest technological innovations in the fashion industry, but some people are looking instead to the hands-on

in the fashion business can be inspired by people who came before them, even if they do not know them personally, because it is a creative industry. You can find a designer whose work you admire or a company whose methods of doing business you admire. I get calls from students regularly asking if they can be an intern or if I can mentor them. I know how hard the fashion business is and the hours involved and the dedication involved. So before I take someone on I really have to see from them that kind of dedication and appreciation for the business. The one thing about fashion and apparel that is really important is that people have to wear clothes, so there's all aspects of it—there's work wear, there's casual wear, there's true high fashion (haute couture)—there are all levels in the fashion business. Apparel is not just haute couture—it is also other very serviceable kinds of apparel that you can wear and use. So that does not mean you have to be talented enough to be the next Yves Saint Laurent or the next Donna Karan—people can get involved in this business with some modicum of talent and just a passion for textiles and sewing and apparel and construction.

Have you always had an interest in fashion?
From the time I was a young girl I learned to sew—my mom taught me to sew, and I learned to make patterns, and I learned to make my own clothes, which I did in junior high and high school and college. In fact, I put myself through two years of school by sewing for other people, doing custom work and so on. It is always been a passion of mine.

What advice would you give to someone who wants to succeed in the fashion business?
I would say the fashion and design business can benefit from people who are artistic, who are willing to pick up a pencil and draw and be creative. I think young people need a broad sense of the business—the creative side and the business side. People are going to always want to wear clothes and surround themselves with beautiful fabrics and textiles in their homes, so it is a business that will always be there. It just may change as technology changes, but there will always be jobs available in our business.

craftsmanship of the past for design inspiration. Patricia Nugent, the textile archivist interviewed in this chapter, says she is beginning to notice designers rejecting the flatness of CAD-generated patterns and print designs in favor of those that show "the depth and the layering and the richness that comes from the feeling of the human hand." Nugent reports, "People are coming to me now and saying, 'Do you have any prints which were actually drawn by a person? Do you have any prints that have the elements of the human hand in them?'" All the more reason for aspiring designers and textile artists to be sure they well versed in the traditional, hands-on aspects of the business, even while they are learning about the latest technologies.

Downsized Fashion Shows

In response to the 2008–2009 economic climate, fewer fashion houses mounted full-scale runway shows to present their collections for Fall 2009. Big shows are enormously costly and offer no guarantee of returns. Instead, some designers opted to present their collections in more intimate and offbeat settings. Patricia Fields debuted the Gerlan Jeans collection in her own home in the Manhattan's Bowery. Actors David Arquette and Courteney Cox hosted a fashion show for the label Propr in their backyard in Los Angeles. The avant-garde designers of the Conscious Designers Collective have taken to staging renegade Roving Catwalk shows, where they simply commandeer a stretch of pavement to showcase their latest designs. It remains to be seen whether this trend will inspire lasting changes in the way that younger and more avant-garde designers, in particular, choose to present their work in the future, regardless of the health of the economy.

Growth in International E-commerce

Fashion e-tailers in the United States have shown a greater willingness to pursue foreign customers. Recent developments such as increased Internet use in Europe, growing support from shipping management companies, as well as PayPal's launch of a new micro-site called the Global Selling Guide—designed to help small business sell their wares abroad—will help drive this trend. In October 2008, the first annual Global E-Commerce Summit was held in Amsterdam.

Major Players and Industry Forces

The fashion industry has undergone many changes in the last few decades, but over the years the types of "movers and the shakers" in the fashion industry have remained, for the most part, the same—with one important exception. Those who command the most power and make the critical decisions about the direction that the industry takes are the top designers in the field, the editors of the fashion media, and the consumers who buy the clothes. The latest major players in the industry are celebrities—usually actors, but also people in music and other fields of entertainment—who have recently come to wield enormous power in the world of fashion.

Top Designers

Any list of top designers, whose work generates billions of dollars for the industry (both directly and via knockoffs) and whose design influence and business acumen continue to shape what comes down catwalks in fashion centers across the globe, would have to include Miuccia Prada.

Since 1989, Prada has reigned as head designer of the company her grandfather Mario founded in 1913. Under her guiding hand, the Prada brand has become synonymous with luxury and status, recognized the world over. In addition to the now-iconic handbag, the Prada signature look features a subdued palette of neutral colors: blacks, grays, browns, and blues. Besides quality and opulence, Prada accessories and fashions reflect the idiosyncratic sensibility of the designer, who has always ignored trends and followed her own instincts. After a Fall 2008 Prada show, Elizabeth Saltzman, the fashion director of *Vanity Fair* magazine, declared that "Everyone else is doing Prada, and everything else looks old next to her."

When *Time* magazine published its annual list of the 100 Most Influential People in the World in May 2009, the only fashion designer to make the cut was Stella McCartney. The 37-year-old daughter of former Beatle Paul McCartney and his late wife, Linda Eastman, the designer made a name for herself when she succeeded Karl Lagerfeld as chief designer at the Paris fashion house Chloé. In 2001, she teamed with Gucci to start her own eponymous line. McCartney's ultra-feminine and ethereal creations are favored by A-list celebrities such as Gwyneth Paltrow, Victoria Beckham (aka Posh Spice), and Liv Tyler. Known for her commitment to ethical fashion, McCartney does not use leather or fur in her designs.

On the menswear front, it is hard to find a designer who has been more influential than Tom Ford, the creative director of Gucci from 1994 to 2004. Ford, a former actor and model, helped make the Gucci label a byword for a kind of dangerous and sexy modern glamour. He then went on to revitalize Yves Saint Laurent. Ford launched his own fashion and beauty empire in 2006.

The first British designer ever appointed to lead a French fashion house, Givenchy, the prodigiously talented John Galliano became chief designer of Christian Dior in 1996. Known for staging outrageous spectacles on the runway, Galliano continues to inject a theatricality and excitement into contemporary fashion with his provocative and intricately constructed designs. In addition to Dior, Galliano runs his own label and produces six couture and ready-to-wear collections a year. His gowns often grace the red carpet at the Academy Awards and Golden Globes.

American designer Donna Karan has built a fashion empire on the basic principles of flexibility and practicality. Karan's line of sophisticated, comfortable, and flattering clothing for urban professional women embodied not just a type of customer but her entire lifestyle. Karan's DKNY line, launched in 1989, made her more casual designs affordable to younger women who could not afford couture prices. By 1992, Donna Karan New York totaled 14 divisions, which included lingerie, men's and children's wear, fragrance, accessories, and body care products, and grossed $275 million. Karan has been Voted Best Woman Designer in the World and Best American Designer to Emerge in 20 Years.

Other current top designers who help make the fashion industry what it is today include the design team of Dolce and Gabbana, Rei Kawakubo of Commes des Garçons, Vera Wang, Alexander McQueen, Karl Lagerfeld of Chanel, Giorgio Armani, Ralph Lauren, and Marc Jacobs, to name just a few.

Fashion Media

While many top designers are men, the vast majority of fashion editors are women. In the front row of the most important fashion shows, you will likely find Anna Wintour, editor in chief of *Vogue* for more than two decades, Cindi Leive of *Glamour* (who some fashion insiders consider even more influential that Wintour), Roberta (Robbie) Myers of *Elle*, *Cosmopolitan*'s Kate White, and Charla Lawhon, editor of *InStyle*. A magazine such as *Glamour* boasts a circulation of 2.4 million, and its Web site attracts close to a million users. With access to this many readers, powerful fashion editors can dictate trends and boost—or destroy—the careers of up-and-coming designers.

The Almighty Consumer

While top designers and fashion editors wield enormous influence in the fashion industry, the most powerful voice in the business may belong to the consumer. A collection that wows the front-row

On the Cutting Edge

Menswear, Women's Wear, Software

The advent of new software in fashion has not only impacted the designer's job but nearly all aspects of the industry, from manufacturing to retail sales to security. Examples of new software that is changing the way people in fashion work include:

- **POS:** Point of Sale Software designed for the retail industry—among other applications, it can help retailers make correct merchandising decisions using correct and timely data.

- **PDM:** Product Development Management—a tool that accumulates all product-related information on a centralized database, it is used to develop clothing lines and manage various aspects of the fashion design business.

- **ERP:** Enterprise Resource Planning Software—a business strategy that helps apparel companies manage purchasing, inventory, suppliers, customer service, and order tracking.

- **RFID:** radio frequency identification—allow for the tracking of products from fiber to final consumer.

audience at a fashion event and wins a four-color, glossy spread in the pages of *Elle* magazine may still languish on the racks—if consumers do not embrace a design it will quickly find its way to the discount bin.

Celebrities

Most recently, the fashion industry has witnessed the rise of the celebrity, a rarified being who has supplanted the supermodel nearly everywhere but on the runway itself. Models on the covers of fashion magazines are rare these days, having been replaced by young and beautiful actresses and singers such as Scarlett Johansson and Beyoncé. The perfume and cosmetics spokesmodel job has also been taken over by celebrities such as Charlize Theron, the "new face" of Dior perfume, and Halle Berry for Revlon. Interviews and photo ops with celebrities on the red carpet before awards shows center around the question of "Who are you wearing?" If an actress makes an appearance in a gown by a lesser known designer and does not wind up in the "What Was She Thinking?" section of the magazine, sales of a particular designer's apparel can skyrocket. Some celebrities have also made inroads into the designing business by starting their own clothing labels, though some of these—such as Sarah Jessica Parker's well-received Bitten and collections from tennis star Venus Williams, actress Amanda Bynes, and rapper/actor LL Cool J—were casualties of the 2008 recession. Celebrity blogs attract thousands of viewers, and one picture of a star wearing a favorite jacket by a new designer can generate plenty of sales.

One celebrity whose foray into fashion has proven enormously successful is music producer Sean "P. Diddy" Combs. Combs's Sean John line of sportswear debuted in 1998, riding the wave of hip-hop fashion that brought the edgy urban street style to the runways. The Sean John brand, which has since expanded to include more upscale men's suits, women's wear, footwear, and fragrance, became a critical and commercial success, and revenues from the brand now exceed $125 million annually. In 2004, Combs received the CFDA Men's Designer of the Year award—the Oscar of fashion—beating out top designers Ralph Lauren and Michael Kors.

Other influential insiders in the fashion world include Peter Marino, an architect of retail spaces; Terry Lundgren, CEO of Federated Department Stores; the vintage dealer Mary Catalina; Marc Ecko, the founder of Ecko Unlimited, a fashion and lifestyle company targeted at young men and women; Julie Gilhart, the fashion director of Barneys New York; and Fern Mallis, senior vice president of fashion at IMG Fashion. IMG is the world's largest producer of fashion events, in addition to running a top international modeling agency and producing an industry-leading event publication for fashion insiders along with fashion-related media programming. Mallis, a self-proclaimed stage mother to designers, presides over Mercedes-Benz Fashion Week, which occurs twice a year in NYC and generates over $235 million for the city each season.

Major Trade Associations in the Fashion Industry

Employers and employees in the U.S. fashion industry are represented by many trade organizations.

The American Apparel and Footwear Association (AAFA) is the national trade organization representing apparel, footwear, and other sewn products companies and their suppliers. AAFA's mission is to promote and enhance its members' competitiveness, productivity, and profitability in the global market.

The Council of Fashion Designers of America (CFDA) is a not-for-profit trade association of over 250 of America's top fashion and accessory designers. The CFDA hosts the annual CFDA Fashion Awards, which recognize excellence in the fashion industry and related arts.

Fashion Group International is a global nonprofit that represents all areas of fashion, apparel, accessories, beauty, and home industries, with over 6,000 members. The group was founded in 1928 by 17 women in the industry and continues to be operated primarily by women.

The National Retail Federation is the world's largest retail trade association. Its members include department stores; specialty, discount, catalog, Internet, and independent retailers; and businesses that provide goods and services to retailers.

Labor Unions

Workers in the apparel industry are represented by UNITE HERE, a union formed by the 1995 merger of the International Ladies Garment Workers Union (ILGWU) and the Amalgamated Clothing and Textile Workers Union (ACTW) into UNITE (Union of Needletrades, Industrial, and Textile Employees), and UNITE's subsequent 2004 merger with HERE (Hotel Employees and Restaurant Employees International Union). UNITE created the "Behind the Label" campaign as part of its effort to eradicate sweatshops in the industry and to raise awareness about working conditions for garment workers. Companies such as Brooks Brothers, Liz Claiborne, Calvin Klein, and Levi Strauss & Co. run "union shops," where employees are guaranteed agreed-upon wages, benefits, and safe working conditions, but in many other apparel companies employees are not unionized.

Major Fashion Industry Events

The fashion business hosts many important industry events each year all over the world—and organizing these events constitutes a huge industry in itself. In the United States, the most famous fashion event is *New York Fashion Week* (recently branded Mercedes-Benz

Fashion Week), which has been held in New York City since 1943. The semiannual event has been staged at Bryant Park since 1993, but will relocate to Lincoln Center's Damrosch Park beginning in 2010. Famous fashion centers such as London, Milan, Paris, Barcelona, and Hong Kong, and many other major cities, all host their own versions of Fashion Week as well. These industry events provide the opportunity for design houses to display their latest collections on the runways and for fashion buyers to check out the designs coming down the catwalk. In fashion capitals such as New York and Paris, these semiannual events showcase designers' fall and winter collections (which are shown during the first months of the year), and their spring and summer collections (which are shown September through November). Some cities' fashion weeks feature specific types of apparel, such as menswear, swimwear, bridal, and couture.

World Fashion Week, which debuted in Los Angeles in 2007, is seven-day Olympic-style event. Other industry events of note include the International Fashion Expo and Conference, Annual Pratt Institute Fashion Show (in New York), the L.A. International Textile Show, the Fashion Career Expo, and the semiannual Women's Wear Daily Fashion Expo.

Chapter 3

On the Job

The majority of jobs in the fashion industry may be grouped into three general categories, identified in this chapter as *fashion design production, merchandising and marketing*, and *media and promotions*. A sampling of positions in the industry that fall outside of these groupings are profiled at the conclusion of the chapter.

Fashion Design Production

The creation of a single item in the fashion industry takes a whole team of professionals, many of whom work behind the scenes to help shape and refine the designer's vision.

Accessory Designer

Accessory designers conceptualize and create designs for jewelry, handbags, shoes, ties, belts, hats, and gloves, to go with clothing. Accessory designers usually specialize in a specific line of accessories directed toward a particular kind of customer such as men, women, children, moms, brides, and so on. They must be familiar with trends in their own specialty as well as in apparel and fabric markets, in order to complement the hottest new styles. Pay levels for accessory designers vary greatly, depending on the types of accessories they produce. For example, a beginning freelance accessory designer might be paid $1,000 for a set number of pieces, in comparison to what Kate Spade makes for a handbag. They often begin in entry-level positions as design assistants or as freelance accessory designers, then move up to associate staff accessory designer, and finally to the position of accessory designs director.

This is a highly competitive field that requires a lot of self-motivation. There are not many staff positions available, so most accessory designers work independently. If you can create industry buzz around your product—have Sarah Jessica Parker photographed wearing your necklace, for instance—you might stand to make a lot of money. While a bachelor's degree in art, fashion design, or fashion merchandising is helpful in this field, it is not required. You will definitely need a portfolio of original self-designed and manufactured products, and a record of successfully marketing and selling those products will make you a far more viable candidate.

Accessory designers need to be highly creative. Technical skill in working with materials is required, as are persistence and determination, the ability to work independently, drawing and sketching skills, knowledge of and ability to react to current fashion trends, knowledge of manufacturing and production processes, and the proven abilities to keep production within a tight budget and to handle stress due to deadlines.

Everyone Knows

Collaboration

While the character of Miranda Priestly, played by Meryl Streep in the film *The Devil Wears Prada*, has contributed to the public perception of fashion editors as being tyrants in high heels, the truth is that this position is, by necessity, a collaborative one. Someone who cannot work well with others is generally not someone who is going to last. Fashion editors team up with stylists, creative directors, photographers, art directors, among others, to produce each issue of a magazine, and an editor must be able to work effectively with all of them.

Artwork Designer

The artwork designer aids the creative director in designing and preparing packaging for an item according to the vision and fashion philosophy of the customer, such as an apparel or accessory designer or a retail establishment. The artwork designer is responsible for making sure that the artwork correctly reflects the customer's marketing strategy correctly, incorporates ongoing customer specifications and modifications, and that it is completed according to schedule. The artwork designer must create a full set of specifications to aid the designer in communicating instructions to the factory during production. Administrative work for this position includes managing, updating, and archiving administrative documents pertaining to the designer's and creative director's decisions.

Clothing Pattern Maker

Clothing patternmakers create full-size fiberboard patterns for clothing. Pattern makers rely on their expertise in body proportions and their understanding of fabric to translate a designer's sketches for a garment into its various pattern pieces. Pattern makers often serve as liaisons between the design and manufacturing groups that are creating a specific clothing line. Pattern makers sometimes move up into positions as designers, or they may be promoted into manufacturing or production management positions.

Creative Director

The creative director (sometimes called the design director or creative manager) functions as the project manager in the fashion industry. Creative directors are responsible for managing the design teams, scheduling fittings and design stages, managing design process flow, and keeping an active communication line with all sectors of the company. The creative director interacts daily with designers, editors and copywriters, and the marketing department in order to meet deadlines at each stage of the production process. Creative directors need to be highly efficient and dynamic since they work in incredibly fast-paced, high-pressure environments.

Dressmaker/Tailor

Dressmakers and tailors have been around far longer than fashion designers. People in these professions are expert sewers who make custom (or bespoke) garments and do apparel alterations and repairs. Dressmakers may specialize in a particular type of garment, such as wedding gowns, and tailors may make tailored suits. They may own their own businesses or work for specialty clothing shops or boutiques, dry cleaners, or large department stores. A dressmaking or tailoring shop can be started up with a relatively small investment. Body scanning technologies may eventually cut back on the need for people in these professions, however.

Dressmakers and tailors take their customers' measurements, construct apparel, perhaps conduct one or more fitting sessions with the customer, and finish the garment. Sometimes they follow commercially made patterns, and sometimes they construct one on the basis of a picture or a sketch. Dressmakers and tailors need to have experience in patternmaking, draping, and other professional skills of clothing construction.

You can take vocational or trade school courses in fashion design, pattern making, sewing and tailoring, and textiles to prepare to work in this field. Some learn the trade while working as an apprentice with an expert tailor or dressmaker.

If you are interested in this job you must have excellent sewing and tailoring skills. You must understand form, proportion, fit, and color and have an excellent fashion sense in order to help clients look their best. You will need to have excellent manual dexterity and be able to work quickly and accurately.

Fabric Designer

Fabric designers develop the fabrics that apparel manufacturers will want for their new lines. Fabric companies hire designers who have artistic ability and technical knowledge about fabric construction. In small fabric mills that do not employ a fashion director, the fabric designer may be responsible for making fashion decisions. In larger companies, fashion decisions regarding fabric choices involve thousands of yards of material, so fabrics must be developed that will fall within a specific price category.

Fabric Structural Designers

Fabric structural designers interpret the advice of their company's fashion department to create new woven or knitted patterns or to redesign patterns that already exist. Much of this work used to be done by hand, involving calculated drawings on graph paper, but now computer programs accomplish these tasks, which include creating designs, showing the fabric structure, and controlling the weaving loom or knitting machine that produces the fabric. A sample of the new fabric must be produced and approved before large quantities are manufactured. Fabric structural designers must have technical expertise in the processes and equipment used to manufacture fabric.

Fabric Surface Designers

Fabric surface designers are responsible for translating a company's color choices and applied print looks on to fabrics. They may specialize as print/repeat artists, colorists, or strike-off artists. The print/repeat artist creates an original textile surface design, or motif, either by hand or on the computer using CAD programs. That motif will be combined repeatedly to create a continuous pattern. Colorists have to work different color combinations for fabric designs. A colorist may recolor a preexisting design for a new seasonal line, or adapt designs for specific customers or markets. The same design motif may be produced in a range of colors and color combinations. Colors are checked on the computer before the final versions are printed on fabrics. After the motifs and colors of a fabric design have been established, strike-off artists arrange prints on the fabric. She or he interprets the intentions of the surface design department to the plant that produces the fabric. Sometimes the strike-off artist must make changes and adjustments to colors or designs because of quality or production restraints.

Fabric mills, textile converters, and vertically integrated garment producers that make their own fabrics need fabric surface designers, usually those with CAD skills. These jobs may also be found at fabric design studios, trend forecasting services, retail private-label product development offices, interior decorating fabric companies, and computer graphics designer firms. Those seeking work in this field need a portfolio that demonstrates a range of artistic skills, including knowledge of related software programs.

Fabric Librarian

Most manufactured fiber companies, natural fiber trade associations, and home sewing pattern companies maintain a fabric library. The fabric librarian is the person responsible for this collection. Fabric swatches are attached to cards on which are recorded detailed information such as the fabric and its source, and these cards are organized and stored in the fabric library. The fabric librarian must be very knowledgeable about textiles and able to discuss fashion trends, fibers, and fabrics with fabric and apparel designers and manufacturers.

Fabric Stylist

A fabric stylist serves as the interface between the creative and business departments of a company, and is responsible for coordinating fabric design, production, and sales. This high-level position requires a knowledge of textiles, long-range planning, fabric design, all aspects of the fashion industry, and the consumer market. A company's sales may depend upon how successfully the fabric stylist can gauge demand and stimulate interest in new fabrics. That person guides the production staff at the textile plant to ensure that they produce the fabric in the right quantities, since any errors can be very costly. Applicants for this job should have many years of textile industry experience.

Each season, fabric stylists organize fabrics into lines, grouping them to be shown and sold to customers. Color cards and swatches are put together for sales presentations in the company's show-

Best Practice

Building a Writing Portfolio

If you are interested in working as a fashion editor but you do not have any previously published work, do not worry. Lots of startup magazines and journals in different fields are looking for writers (check on Craigslist or Freelancewritinggigs.com, for instance) but cannot afford to pay much (or anything) for their work. You can offer to write articles on subjects that interest you, and when the piece is published, you will have a writing sample for your file.

room. They may also be sent to potential customers, such as apparel designers and manufacturers, who will then order enough fabric to create samples of their new designs. The fabric stylist uses feedback from these customers to create promotional materials, which are sent to the fashion press, retailers, and consumers.

Individuals interested in this line of work often start as assistants to the stylist. (This job should not be confused with that of assistant stylist, a middle management position in large fabric firms of textile design companies. The assistant stylist works with the stylist to compile lines, prepares storyboards, and gives assignments to fabric designers.) Assistants to the stylist usually set up appointments for the stylist and do clerical work. Sometimes assistants act as go-betweens with the company's plants or textile mills, or they may meet with customers in the stylist's absence.

Fashion Designer

Fashion designers (also called apparel designers) conceptualize and create new clothing and accessory designs. They analyze fashion trends and work closely with production, marketing, and sales departments to design, produce, and promote a finished, ready-to-wear product for apparel manufacturers, specialty and retail stores, and individual clients. Fashion designers usually specialize in a specific line of clothing. In larger fashion houses, individual designers may work in very specialized areas such as T-shirts, evening dresses, or maternity clothes. Some experienced designers are required to travel to promote their fashion lines. Potential employers include retailers, haute couturiers, textile and apparel manufacturers, and fashion studios.

Some of the best opportunities for fashion designers exist in wholesale companies as well as mass-market design firms. Designers must be willing to work long hours during crunch periods and to also deal with seasonal slowdowns.

A person interested in this job would do well to have a two- or four-year degree in fashion design, fashion merchandising, or a related field. A degree helps to start building a portfolio and often helps with the networking that is so important in this field. However, a degree is not absolutely required. Several years as an intern, junior designer, or design assistant is worthwhile, in order to help build up a professional design portfolio. Fashion designers need to be able to distinguish between colors and to judge fabric quality; in addition, they need a knack for creative expression; sewing, drawing, and sketching skills; computer skills (especially CAD); knowledge of fashion trends and forecasts; persistence; understanding of manufacturing and production processes; and a good eye for style, shape, and color. Also helpful are the abilities to deal with ambiguity and rejection and to handle stress due to deadlines, as are good business and marketing skills.

Individuals interested in becoming fashion designers generally begin as design assistants. They can move up to assistant designer, then associate designer, then fashion director.

Problem Solving

A Public Pledge

The secret was out. In 2006, Limited Brands, the parent company of Victoria's Secret, had a big problem on its hands. The well-known manufacturer of lingerie—which mails out more than 350 million glossy catalogs a year—was getting a lot of pressure from the environmental activist group ForestEthics to stop printing its catalogs on paper made from endangered forests in Canada. ForestEthics targeted the company's image with ads featuring lingerie-wearing models wielding chainsaws. What was shaping up to be a public relations nightmare ultimately turned out to be a great PR opportunity for the company. By publicly pledging to use a more sustainable source for its paper, Limited Brands was able to avoid a tremendous amount of negative press and potential damage to its brand and show its customers that Victoria's Secret is a company that cares about the earth. That is a win-win situation.

Fashion Merchandiser

Fashion merchandisers, also called merchandisers or apparel merchandisers, who work on the apparel production side of the industry (versus the retail side; see below), track and analyze market trends, production costs, and previous sales numbers to determine the product direction that manufacturers will take each season. If wide-shouldered jackets are going to be the next big thing, the fashion merchandiser needs to be one of the first to spot the trend. Fashion merchandisers on the retail side have to track consumer trends and the latest styles to determine store inventory and to price clothes. They arrange the receiving and storage of apparel, and supervise the creation of visual displays and the overall look of the retail environment. They may also be responsible for keeping track of profits and losses. Merchandisers have some of the more important jobs within an apparel company, and they have large bottom line and personnel management responsibilities, and the chance to advance to high-paying positions.

Fashion merchandisers work in fashion salons, fashion consulting firms, department stores, specialty shops and boutiques, for fashion magazines, and in import and export firms. Useful personal traits for someone in this line of work include an extensive knowledge of the apparel industry, strong math skills and analytical ability, and the abilities to predict trends, make smart product-line decisions, and work with other executives and stay cool under pressure.

Preparation for an entry-level assistant merchandiser includes a two-year associate's degree in fashion merchandising, with courses in subjects such as consumer research, CAD, and the culture and history of fashion. A more advanced position typically requires a four-year bachelor's degree in fashion merchandising, fashion design, apparel production, or marketing. An MBA is an advantage, as is time spent in an executive training program.

The work experience required to rise in merchandising is 5 to 10 years spent in the apparel industry, along with some retail or sales experience. Fashion merchandisers often start out as retail management trainees and work their way up to fashion buyer or a merchandising assistant position.

Fashion Sales Representative

Fashion sales representatives sell a manufacturer's garments and accessories to fashion buyers from wholesale and retail stores. They usually solicit orders from new and prospective customers within a designated geographical area. They show samples, illustrations, and catalogs of their manufacturer's product line. They must be well informed about the products they represent and ready to answer any questions about them. They listen to customer's concerns and complaints about the product and help resolve problems. They also help their customers to sell the product line by arranging events such as trunk shows and in-store fashion shows. Fashion sales reps usually travel a lot, sometimes internationally.

Sales reps often have a chance to increase their earnings through commissions on sales they make or bonuses for their performance. Outlooks for these positions are very good, especially if an applicant is willing to travel or relocate for the job. A bachelor's degree in fashion merchandising, business, or marketing is helpful, though not necessary. Previous experience in sales is also an advantage. Successful sales reps should be personable, have excellent written and oral communication skills, and be enthusiastic about the product line that they represent. They also need to be self-motivated, able to handle rejection, and are required to demonstrate knowledge of industry trends and manufacturer's competitors.

A successful fashion sales rep can work his or her way up to sales manager, regional sales manager, national sales manager, and finally to vice president of sales.

Pattern Grader

Also called a grader, this person is responsible for reducing or enlarging a pattern created by a pattern maker in order to produce clothes across a range of sizes (such as small, medium, and large) and fits (petite or tall). Pattern graders may use charts, machinery, or computer software programs such as Fashion CAD and PolyPattern in their work. Pattern grading is generally considered a more technically oriented career than patternmaking or designing. Pattern graders may work directly for design houses or manufacturers, or for firms that specialize in pattern grading. Experience as a pattern grader may lead to a job as a production manager. Anyone applying for this job is expected to have at least a two-year degree in patternmaking technology, fashion design, or a related field. Previous experience with patternmaking software is a plus, and good pattern graders possess drafting and math skills and are good with their hands. Analytical and problem-solving skills are helpful, as are the abilities to handle multiple projects at once and to meet deadlines.

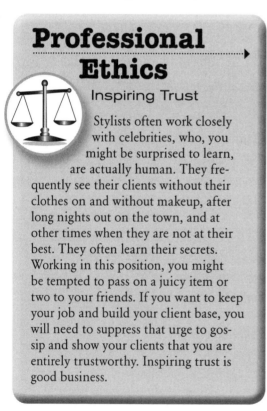

Professional Ethics

Inspiring Trust

Stylists often work closely with celebrities, who, you might be surprised to learn, are actually human. They frequently see their clients without their clothes on and without makeup, after long nights out on the town, and at other times when they are not at their best. They often learn their secrets. Working in this position, you might be tempted to pass on a juicy item or two to your friends. If you want to keep your job and build your client base, you will need to suppress that urge to gossip and show your clients that you are entirely trustworthy. Inspiring trust is good business.

Product Developer

A product developer works either during the design stages of apparel or accessory production or at the production line. At the pre-launch stage, the product developer further develops the fashioned product based on the customer's merchandise plan with the goal of increasing its commercial value. Like the designer, a product developer is expected to research market trends and to monitor the performance of similar products on the market. She or he must also source for the materials and make sure that the design evolves commercially during the process of product development. Product developers usually work with a development team to which they delegate many of the tasks required to make sure that project deadlines are met. Product developers who work at the production line are responsible for monitoring and, if necessary, redirecting the production process to ensure that the final product adheres to the commercial and technical specifications provided by the customer. They also must provide industrial support to all suppliers and the merchandising team and must make sure that all quality standards are being consistently met. They work with suppliers in the case of technical queries, follow up factory production of sample garments and bulk orders, and continuously monitor production cost levels. Anyone applying for this position needs to have a minimum of five years in production and to have a thorough understanding of the process flow. Excellent communication skills are an asset, since product developers must communicate constantly with suppliers, many of them overseas.

Product Manager

This is a relatively senior position within a manufacturer's organization. Also called a product development manager, product managers are responsible for overseeing the conceptualization, design, construction, selling, and distribution of a manufacturer or designer's product. They also have to oversee the setup and implementation of quality assurance protocols for that product. A product manager is typically responsible for a specific product or line.

A product manager typically works up to the position, beginning as a market analyst and moving up to merchandiser before being promoted. Product managers may advance to the position of director of product management.

Anyone interested in this position must have a bachelor's degree in business administration, marketing, or apparel production. An MBA is an advantage, as is involvement in an executive training program. From 5 to 10 years of experience in apparel development or product management is required, and it is important to have strong math and analytical skills along with thorough knowledge of the apparel business. Product managers also need to be well organized, decisive, and able to handle pressure well.

Product Line Manager

At the production line, a product line manager's job is to see that a whole range of products are manufactured in a systematic order, from the product development stages to mass production. At the sampling stages, the product line manager must create a one-off product with the same design specifications as the final product. On the basis of this sample, the product line manager and the merchandising team will present target prices and recommended retail pricing. She or he will be responsible for ensuring the quality of the product is proportional to its delivery performance. This job typically requires a master's degree in clothing technology or manufacturing, or a similar degree from a textile school, along with a minimum of three years experience in product development, line management, or marketing. Good communication skills are also a requirement.

Sample Workers

A sample is trial garment or prototype that is made up exactly as it will look when it is manufactured and sold to the retailer. A sample cutter follows a pattern to cut out the various parts needed to construct a sample garment. A sample maker, also called a sample hand, follows the designer's pattern, sketch, and specifications to sew the sample garment together. Sample makers must be trained in all clothing construction and finishing techniques and be able to follow someone else's sketches and specifications precisely and accurately.

Showroom Sales Representative

Showroom sales representatives work at manufacturer's or designer's offices, where they meet with visiting fashion buyers and show the latest product lines and demonstrate their features. Once the fashion buyer agrees to purchase the products, the showroom sales rep must accurately write up the buyer's order. They are then responsible for making sure that the correct quantities of the correct items arrive on time, in saleable condition, at their customer's stores. During market weeks and fashion weeks, showroom sales reps often work long hours. Like fashion sales reps, they can improve their earnings via commissions on sales and bonuses based on their performance.

Forecasters predict there will be many of these positions available. College graduates with outgoing personalities and good communication skills have an excellent chance of being hired as showroom sales assistants. Previous sales experience is a plus, as well as a degree in fashion merchandising, business, or marketing. If you are applying for a job as a showroom sales rep, you should be knowledgeable about the manufacturing and retail sectors of the fashion industry and have good organizational and computer skills. Possibilities for advancement with this job include ultimately moving up to a position as a showroom sales manager.

Sketcher

Fashion firms sometimes hire sketchers to do freehand drawings of apparel ideas that designers have draped on to mannequins with fabric. Sketchers translate other's three-dimensional ideas into two-dimensional form. They need to be able to draw quickly, with precision and accuracy.

Sketching assistants may be employed by large manufacturing firms and commercial pattern companies to make detailed drawings of fashion ideas. They have to sketch designs for different types of apparel in precise, technical detail and point out various construction and design features on the garments. They "swatch" their sketches by attaching fabric and trim samples. They also fill out specification sheets, which are detailed accounts of the construction details for each item. This job requires training in fashion illustration or art. Applicants for this job need to be able to present a portfolio of their artwork.

Sourcing Director

A sourcing director must oversee, manage, and provide strategic direction for all aspects of sourcing. He or she evaluates whether or not existing manufacturing facilities are in compliance with various

On the Cutting Edge

An Ongoing Debate

Following the deaths of several severely underweight models, organizers of the 2006 Madrid Fashion Week enacted the world's first ban on super-thin models, requiring that models who appear on Spain's runways have a BMI (body mass index) of more than 18.5. The ruling prompted a storm of opposition from the fashion industry, which pressured organizers of London Fashion Week to scrap its proposed ban on ultra-thin models from the catwalks. In response, the agency that finances that event threatened to withdraw funding if underweight models were allowed on the runway. This is an ongoing debate in the industry, so watch for more news in the future.

laws and regulations, and researches, evaluates, and secures new manufacturing resources. Sourcing directors must be fully versed in international customs laws and Standard Manufacturing Processes. As the leader of all sourcing managers, the sourcing director also provides leadership to customers and suppliers in order to maintain control of the merchandise programs, which need to be sourced on tight schedules and within profit margin targets. A sourcing director should have a minimum of 10 years' work experience in global sourcing, a minimum of a bachelor's degree, a strong understanding of manufacturing and supply chain process and functions, strong management and negotiation skills, and demonstrated leadership abilities.

Technical Designer, Apparel

A technical designer for apparel executes design sketches exclusively on a computer, using software programs such as Fashion CAD and StyleDraper Pro. This is a great way to make money, be a part of the design process, and work in the fashion industry.

Trend Forecaster

Trend forecasters start their work as much as two years before the fashion season. Their predictions influence everything from fabrics and trims, to textures, silhouettes, and colors that are eventually featured in the designers' collections. Trend presentations are given at least twice a year at venues like New York's Fashion Institute of

Technology, and are attended by hundreds of designers and product developers. High-profile trend forecasters include Li Edelkoort of Trend Union and David Wolfe of D3.

Merchandising and Marketing

Beyond the design of a garment or accessory, the retail end of the business requires professionals of all backgrounds and skill sets to help get products into the hands of the consumer. They thereby help fashion fulfill its role as a living, wearable art form.

Boutique Owner

Boutiques are specialty stores that feature items such as dresses, swimwear, lingerie, and accessories. Lots of fashion school graduates dream about opening their own boutiques, but setting up your own business typically requires a large initial investment and a combination of creativity, drive, and business smarts. You may have to obtain a bank loan or use your savings to cover startup costs, and losses are usually expected in the first few years until the venture gets off the ground. Successful boutique owners usually have an in-depth knowledge of the fashion retail industry as well an ability to handle all the elements involved in running a business, such as purchasing inventory, arranging visual displays, bookkeeping, and managing employees. If a store does well, the owner may open up additional branches.

Preparation for this job typically requires a bachelor's degree in business management or fashion retailing, or a related field. If you want to attract investors, it helps to have an MBA and a good business plan. Previous experience in retail sales is a plus, such as working as a stock clerk or as a retail sales associate. Boutique owners are entrepreneurs who need to know about the latest trends and understand the fashion marketplace.

Fashion Buyer

The fashion buyer (also known as an apparel buyer or simply a buyer) uses his or her sense of style, knowledge of trends, and understanding of target customers' need and desires to create an attractive selection of apparel for retail stores. They are responsible for choosing and purchasing apparel and accessories from manufacturers, designers, and wholesalers for retail sale. Buyers often make their purchases up to one or two years in advance, due to the length of time it takes for a designer or a manufacturer to fill an order, so they need to know about the history of fashion trends and to project that knowledge into the future. Buyers also have to budget and plan inventory to ensure that a supply of apparel is always available to the customer.

Buyers work for department stores, wholesale clothing distributors, or smaller retail establishments. Those who work for large department stores generally specialize in a particular line of apparel or accessories.

If you begin work as an assistant buyer, you have a good chance of being promoted to buyer within three to five years. Buyers can eventually advance to the position of divisional merchandise manager.

Preparation to be a buyer typically includes earning a college degree in fashion merchandising or a related field. Coursework in business and fashion design can also be useful, as can retail sales experience. Successful fashion buyers usually have a comprehensive knowledge of fashion history and trends, a good understanding of customers' buying behavior, excellent analytical skills, and the ability to budget, manage inventory, and deal with stress on the job.

Fashion Coordinator

Fashion coordinators, also called fashion directors, are the people who create a unified look across all the fashion divisions of a department store, design house, or fashion magazine. In order to keep up with the latest information in fabric and textile development, they constantly monitor trade publications and talk to designers. Fashion directors have to determine the potential for success of a particular garment or clothing line and figure out the best plan for promotion and marketing. They share this information with retail sales people as well as with the buyers who make inventory purchases.

Fashion coordinators may also be responsible for supervising promotional photo shoots and interfacing with fabric mills, suppliers, and wholesalers to make sure that production is on schedule and that all colors and designs are according to plan. People in this position often travel frequently.

Anyone seeking a position as a fashion coordinator should have at least a bachelor's degree in fashion merchandising or fashion design, though an associate's degree may be sufficient to gain an entry-level job as an assistant fashion coordinator. You will need extensive experience in the industry, usually beginning in retail sales and moving through various merchandising positions such as buyer. Much of the knowledge required for this type of work is gained on the job.

Fashion coordinators usually have an excellent understanding of fashion and fashion trends, an in-depth understanding of consumer behavior, a flair for style, as well as very strong organization and communication skills.

Retail Merchandiser

Retail merchandisers are also known as merchandise managers and fashion merchandisers. Their job is to select, purchase, promote, and sell clothing and accessories for a retail store, department, division, or chain. They keep abreast of fashion trends and visit manufacturers, designers, and merchandise markets and make fashion forecasts based on the information they gather. A retail merchandiser will work with a team of buyers and managers to determine how to best sell their products, including advising the advertising and display departments on how and where to position merchandise. Sometimes retail merchandisers specialize in a particular line of clothing. This job usually requires lots of travel and long hours during certain periods of the year.

In large companies, the retail merchandiser works directly under the divisional merchandise manager (or DMM). A divisional merchandise manager supervises a group of buyers and coordinates the merchandise of related departments, divisions, or stores. This person acts as a liaison between the company's upper management and buyers by presenting and interpreting company merchandising policies. DMMs typically have many years' worth of buying experience, and they advise buyers about budget control, solve problems with vendors, and confer with buyers about changing conditions in the market. DMMs are responsible for overseeing merchandise distribution, and they plan new departments for stores and carry out plans requested by higher level management.

Someone interested in this career track may begin as a buyer, advance to associate merchandising manager, and then to merchandising manager. The senior executive position of general merchandising manager (or GMM) is the person responsible for the total retail merchandising operation.

If you would like to get into this field, you will need a two- or four-year degree in fashion merchandising, fashion design, or a related field. Coursework in business is very helpful, as are classes in merchandise planning, sales, marketing, and promotion. Extensive experience in the retail apparel industry, especially in merchandise buying and retail sales, is a requirement. Individuals who succeed as retail merchandisers have their finger on the pulse of the fashion marketplace and stay informed about designers, consumers, competitors, manufacturers, and products. They need exceptional people-management and time-management skills as well as expertise in pricing, forecasting, product development, and sales.

Retail Store Manager

Retail store managers oversee all aspects of a store's operations. They can be involved in everything from hiring, training, and promoting employees, to approving merchandise displays and advertisements, to ordering a store's merchandise inventory, to establishing pricing policies. Store managers have a lot of responsibility, so they often have to work long hours, evenings, and holidays. Their jobs often depend on how profitable their store is.

Retail store managers often begin their careers as retail sales associates, and then advance to associate managers before becoming store managers. A college degree is required, with coursework in fashion merchandising, fashion retailing, and business management. Candidates with a background in retail sales will be stronger candidates for this position. Large department stores sometimes require employees interested in this career path to participate in in-house managerial training programs.

Store managers must be highly organized and knowledgeable about marketing, accounting, sales, and management. They must also have excellent interpersonal skills.

Visual Merchandiser

Visual merchandisers conceptualize, design, and implement window and in-store displays for retail stores and online retailers. This is a creative job that demands a lot of technical skill—you need to know how best to arrange eye-catching displays of merchandise that use retail space efficiently. Visual merchandisers must create and maintain an image for a department or an entire store that appeals to the retailer's target customers and attracts them to the merchandise.

Also called merchandise display artists or visual display designers, people in these positions may be hired to oversee the design and layout of a store, a fashion showroom, or a tradeshow display. When designing displays, they use their knowledge of customers' buying behavior as well as their understanding of current fashion trends. In large department stores or retail chains, visual merchandisers may work with the head office as well as other design teams (sometimes including buyers and salespeople) to ensure their plans are consistent with a corporation's image or brand.

Requirements for this job are a bachelor's degree in visual or fashion merchandising, graphic design, applied design, or a related field. Coursework in consumer psychology is a plus. A background in retail sales and a firsthand familiarity with consumer behavior is very useful in this field.

From an entry-level position as a visual merchandising assistant, you can advance to the position of visual merchandiser and from there to a visual merchandising coordinator. The top job in the career track is that of visual merchandising director.

Good visual merchandisers are in demand, so the outlook for this job is excellent. Skilled visual merchandisers can have a big impact on a retailer's sales figures.

Media and Promotions

Design and retail create the link between products and consumers, but only through active promotion in various media outlets can fashion trends become recognized, amplified, and ultimately canonized within the culture.

Fashion Editor

Reports about the death of print journalism may be exaggerated, judging by the power wielded by top fashion editors such as *Vogue*'s Anna Wintour, of whom *Time* magazine said: "Runway shows do not start until she arrives. Designers succeed because she anoints them. Trends are created or crippled on her command." Though many of the financial titans in the fashion industry are men, the majority of top-tier fashion editors in chief are women such as Roberta "Robbie" Myers of *Elle* and Linda Wells of *Allure*.

Fashion editors are responsible for supervising the process of creating, developing, and presenting content for fashion magazines

Fast Facts

The Unknown Arbiters

Top designers and supermodels have become household names, but the real movers in the fashion industry are often unknown by people outside the business. Here are some of the most important people you probably have not heard of in fashion:

- **Bernard Arnault**, chairman of the luxury conglomerate LVMH (Moët Hennessy Louis Vuitton) and the most important businessperson in the fashion industry
- **Margaret Hays Adame**, president, Fashion Group International
- **Dr. Valerie Steele**, prolific author and director and chief curator of the Museum at FIT
- **Li Edelkoort**, trend forecaster, Trend Union
- **Nicole Fischelis**, vice president and fashion director, Macy's
- **Didier Grumbach**, president, Fédération Française de la Couture, the world's largest group of fashion trade organizations
- **Ruth Finley**, publisher of the Fashion Calendar since 1941 (yep, that date is not a typo)
- **Simon Doonan**, creative director, Barneys New York
- **Eric and Philip Sauma**, co-owners, Mood Fabrics (of *Project Runway* fame).
- **Candy Pratt Price**, executive fashion director, style.com
- **Julie Mannion**, head of show production, and **Nian Fish**, consulting creative director, KCD Worldwide Staging, responsible for staging huge runway shows

and newspapers, photo shoots, Web sites, or television shows. They report to the editor in chief, and they are responsible for deciding on the creative directions that their departments will pursue during a particular season or issue. Depending on the size of the publication, editors may specialize in areas such as apparel, beauty, footwear, or other accessories.

This type of work is fast-paced and driven by deadlines, and editors often put in long hours when it is time to put out an issue.

A fashion editor may work for a traditional print publication, such as a fashion or lifestyle magazine or a style or fashion section in a newspaper, or she or he may work for online publications, such as a fashion Web site or a style blog, or on a televised fashion program. Recently, there has been lots of growth in Internet-based editorial jobs.

In-house fashion editors hold staff positions in a particular company. They work a nine-to-five job (theoretically at least; they often put in long hours to reach deadlines) at an organization or publication that offers benefits and pays a regular salary. A freelance fashion editor is an independent agent in charge of finding her own clients and projects. Projects are taken on a contract basis and require the fashion editor to gather the apparel and accessories necessary for a given project for a newspaper, magazine, or Internet spread.

Most fashion editors' jobs involve travel to keep up with the latest fashion trends, whether in the United States or overseas, as the fashion industry becomes increasingly globalized. Editors often meet with designers and attend runway shows and industry social functions where members of the fashion press get goody bags filled with perfume and cosmetics, in addition to other perks.

According to the Bureau of Labor Statistics, the employment of writers and editors is predicted to show a 10 percent increase between 2002 and 2012.

Anyone setting out on this career path should have a bachelor's degree in journalism or fashion design and merchandising. The career ladder that leads, ultimately, to the position of editor in chief typically begins with an editorial assistant or an associate editor position, progresses to editor, then to senior editor. A journalism internship at a fashion magazine often provides that first foot in the door and will be a great way to get the real skinny of what the business is like, dispelling any glamorous myths and giving a realistic sense of what the position requires. A portfolio of previous written and published work is usually required to apply to higher-level positions. Anyone looking to advance in this field must combine a love of fashion and a broad knowledge of trends and fashion history with excellent writing and communication skills. You also need to work well with others, perform well under pressure, and be highly organized.

Fashion Illustrator

Fashion illustrators create sketches and drawings of apparel, shoes, and accessories for fashion advertisements, catalogs, and other media. They draw by hand or they use special CAD software to create illustrations. Some fashion illustrators combine handcrafted techniques, such as embroidery and collage, with digital techniques to create entirely new multimedia effects.

Fashion illustrations are used in newspaper and magazine advertising layouts, department store ads, direct mail catalogs, TV commercials, films, brochures, and flyers. Fashion illustrators may find work with pattern companies and fashion forecast firms. Also, full-time jobs are available with clothing catalog companies. Fashion artists often work on a freelance basis, contracting with a given department store or ad agency.

The job has changed as a result of illustrating software such as Adobe Illustrator, and some fashion illustrators work entirely on the computer. During the 1990s, many of the jobs originally done by fashion illustrators were taken by fashion photographers, resulting in these types of jobs becoming more scarce. However, at the end of the twentieth century, innovative illustrators such as Jason Brooks, Graham Rounthwaite, and David Downton helped make this art form current again.

You will not necessarily need a college degree to work in this field, but a degree in art, drawing, fashion illustration, or design can be helpful, since faculty often elect to serve as mentors to aspiring artists. Assembling a strong, well-organized, and edited portfolio of your work is crucial so that you can demonstrate your skill and range. In addition to hand-drawn illustrations, potential clients or employers may also wish you to submit online or electronic samples of your work. You will need to show evidence of excellent computer skills and familiarity with CAD and related software as well as excellent drawing skills and evidence of your creativity. Fashion illustrator Annabelle Verhoye advises: "Develop your own body of work. Put together a portfolio that illustrates your own personality and the type of work that excites you. The keyword here is *passion*. When your work focuses on something deeply felt and earnestly expressed, it will naturally convey its importance and find a home. It will create a powerful connection and become true and compelling for others. Be true to yourself."

Freelance fashion illustrators who have proven themselves may advance to a staff position as an illustrator, with more job security and benefits.

Fashion Photographer

Fashion photographers are hired by magazines, catalogs, Web sites, and design houses to conceptualize, shoot, develop, and print still photos and/or videos to display apparel and accessories in a creative manner that will attract consumers. Highly successful fashion photographers include Irving Penn, Richard Avedon, Mario Testino, and Annie Liebowitz, all of whom worked for *Vogue* magazine. Professional fashion photographers must be skilled at working with models and know how to pose and manipulate them in order to get the best shots. They must have a keen eye for style. Photographers may also be responsible for scouting out interesting locations for photo shoots and for hiring models and assistants, such as fashion stylists, to help with the shoot.

The field of fashion photography is expected to grow as much as 17 percent between 2004 and 2014, according to the U.S. Department of Labor. Growing use of the Internet may spur additional growth in the industry, as Web sites seek to perpetually refresh their content. Most fashion photographers get their start as photo assistants, helping a photographer carry equipment, scout locations for shoots, set up the lighting, and so on. A staff or freelance photographer can advance to the position of photo editor and then to director of photography.

If you are looking to make it as a fashion photographer, you will need a strong portfolio of work that demonstrates skill, versatility, and personal style. When you are building your portfolio, be sure to include some of your own images and projects, not just the assignments you have done for your clients. You will want to demonstrate that you have your own individual point of view, which you will bring to the job you are applying for. On-the-job training in some capacity, whether as an assistant or intern, is essential. A degree in photography or art is not a requirement but it can be a useful way to establish contacts in the field. To do this work you need to have a lot technical knowledge about how different cameras work, about lighting, composition, darkroom procedures, and other matters. You also need good interpersonal skills and the ability to set your subjects and ease and to establish a rapport with them. Knowledge of trends in fashion and in photography can be very useful, as well.

Fashion PR Specialist

Public relations specialists and publicists are hired to help apparel companies and retail stores maintain a favorable public image. They think up innovative ways of keeping a company's brand or a designer's name in the public eye, and in the public favor. PR specialists prepare press releases and schedule press conferences to distribute news through television, newspapers, radio, and direct mail. They also have to interact with the media when questions or conflicts arise, so they have to maintain strong professional relationships with media personnel.

The outlook is excellent for aspirants in this field, since the market for PR specialists working solely in fashion is growing quickly. Most large retailers and fashion houses have their own public relations departments. After three to five years worth of experience, PR specialists can often move into more senior positions, such as PR coordinator.

A four-year degree in public relations is generally considered a basic requirement, and coursework in fashion and journalism can also be helpful. As in most fashion jobs, an internship in a fashion publication or media outlet gives you a distinct advantage, and is an important means of establishing contacts within the industry. Excellent writing and oral communication skills are a requirement of this job, as is an even temperament and an ability to keep cool under pressure. People usually begin in positions as promotions assistants, move up to PR specialist, and then advance to PR coordinator. Director of public relations is the top job in this career path.

Fashion Stylist

Stylists work on photo shoots, fashion magazine layouts, commercial advertisements on television or in print, or music videos. Stylists work with fashion photographers and directors to bring to life a specific vision for the project. Fashion stylists often have to scout for locations and create the mood for a shot by selecting the appropriate props, lighting, accessories, and models for the shoot. They coordinate styles and colors and make sure that all garments are ready for the shoot—sometimes snipping dangling threads and pressing a hem.

Fashion stylists are employed by retailers, catalog publishers, magazines, newspaper, television and film producers, ad agencies, public relations firms, music production companies as well as by individual celebrities or wealthy clients who want to present a polished image for highly publicized events such as award shows. Many stylists have become celebrities in their own right, such as Rachel Zoe, who has her own reality show, *The Rachel Zoe Project*. While some stylists are employed full time, many work on a freelance basis or run their own businesses. Stylist earnings can range from very low to high. Entry-level fashion stylists may average $150 to $200 per day, whereas an experienced stylist can command $5,000 per day. Top-level stylists earn in excess of $100,000 a year.

The career path for this position typically begins with an internship or by being a stylist's apprentice. From there you may move up to assistant fashion stylist and after that to staff fashion stylist. This is a job where networking is paramount—most successful stylists have huge networks of industry contacts. Satisfied clients tend to hire the same stylists again, so once you have done that you must maintain your professional reputation by getting things done on time and within budget. One high-profile celebrity client can make you. People who succeed in the position are very personable and have a great eye for style; they are creative and resourceful, know a lot about trends, are self-motivated, good with their hands, and can demonstrate technical know-how along with business skills.

Fashion Writer

Fashion writers produce editorial copy for media outlets such as fashion magazines, newspapers, fashion Web sites and blogs, and television programming. Most of the industry's fashion writers work within

Fast Facts

Luxury Spending Swoosh Bamboozle

A design student, Carolyn Davidson, created the trademark Nike "swoosh." She was paid $35.

the editorial departments of fashion design firms. Like journalists everywhere, fashion reporters must conduct research and interview sources when preparing articles. According to the U.S. Department of Labor, demand for fashion journalists and writers is expected to grow through 2014, though there is extreme competition for these positions. Fashion writing jobs are concentrated in the industry centers of

New York and California, although freelance fashion writers can live anywhere in the world and submit their content online.

Educational preparation to be a fashion writer usually requires a four-year degree with a focus in fashion journalism or fashion merchandising, which may give you a leg up on the competition. A portfolio of written and published work is important. In addition to a love of fashion and style and a knowledge of the industry and its history, you need very strong writing and editorial skills, as well as attention to detail, fact-checking, and researching skills. An entry-level position as an editorial assistant can lead to a position as a staff fashion writer.

Graphic Designer

Graphic designers or graphic artists design and prepare camera-ready copy for any type of printed material, including advertising, book covers, packaging, brochures, and stationery for fashion businesses. Employers who need graphic designers include fashion magazines, advertising agencies, and graphic design firms. In a large agency, the graphic designer will work on a team that includes the art director and the creative director. Paste-up artists may advance to the position of graphic designer.

Scan any fashion job list and you will see that there are ample opportunities for graphic designers, in part because of the growth of the Internet. Successful graphic designers are highly creative and possess an excellent design sense and proven success with a variety of projects. A graphic designer may advance to become an art director or a creative director, or may open a design firm and hire other graphic designers.

A two- or four-year degree in graphic design or a related field is highly recommended, and a portfolio of previous work is required. Successful graphic designers combine an excellent sense of style, color, and design with creativity and imagination, attention to detail, and the ability to tolerate criticism when the client wants to change or adjust a design. It is a collaborative process, and you cannot let your ego get in the way of the finished product.

Media Buyer

Media buyers are in charge of selecting and buying the best media for their client's ads. They arrange for broadcasting commercials on television and radio, publishing print ads in magazines, trade journals, and newspapers, or mailing promotional materials directly to the public. Media buyers deal with media salespeople, who try to persuade them to buy time on their TV channel or publish an ad in their magazine. Media buyers often use bargaining skills to get the lowest rates and the best ad placement for their clients.

Publicist

Publicists, sometimes called public relations agents, help a company project its public image. They may work for a large retailer or an independent publicity consultant that has been hired by a company to do their PR work. A publicist helps tell the story of a firm and its products through various media. He or she will work to get favorable editorial mentions and photographs of a client in the national media or product "plugs" on broadcasts. Publicists often attend meetings, conferences, and conventions where they speak about products, and they arrange speaking engagements for company officials. This job requires excellent communication skills and may involve travel.

Other Jobs in Fashion

While not intimately involved in design, retail, or promotion, the following positions are no less essential to the continued dynamism of the fashion industry.

Costume Designer

A costume designer, or costumer, creates wardrobes for performers in movies, television shows, stage plays, operas, ballets, circuses, parades, and advertisements. A costumer might be hired by a theater company or a movie or TV studio. Many costumers are freelance designers hired to work with the wardrobing staff on a particular show.

Theatrical costumers work from scripts to create the appropriate clothing for characters in a production. They need to know how to use clothing to project desired moods and effects, and how different lighting conditions influence how costumes appear onstage. Costumers need a solid background in the history of costume and dress, since the clothing they create must be appropriate for certain cultures, time periods, and income levels. Their costume design decisions may be governed by the size and shape of the stage as well as the production's wardrobe budget.

Costume designers may enter the field as costume technicians or wardrobe helpers, whose duties may include researching to make sure that period designs are authentic, shopping for fabrics and props, organizing costumes and accessories for a character and scene, helping the actors dress before a show and between scenes, and caring for wardrobe between performances.

Model

Models use their appearances to persuade consumers to buy the products they advertise. Models work with clothing, makeup, and accessories in a variety of poses and settings. They may model in showrooms, retail stores, custom salons, fashion houses, or specialty stores. Runway models are hired to work in fashion shows, which is a theatrical type of work. Print models pose for the still photographs used in print ads, brochures, and store catalogs. There are specialty models, as well: Body part models may only model their hands, feet, or legs. Plus-size models are sizes 14 and up.

Earning vary, depending on the type of job, the size and the location as well as the popularity of the individual model. Supermodels, such as Kate Moss or Gisele Bündchen, may command upwards of $10,000 per engagement.

The U.S. Department of Labor expects opportunities for models to grow by 10 to 20 percent between 2002 and 2012, with an increasing demand for both male and female models who are representative of diverse racial and ethnic groups. This is a competitive field, attracting many people with its glamorous and high-profile nature. Successful models often go on to have successful careers in the fashion business or in entertainment.

You do not need a college degree to become a model, but a background in theater or dance can be helpful, along with coursework in art and fashion design. Most employers prefer some previous modeling experience or training, and a portfolio of your previous work is essential for landing "go-sees" and jobs. Be sure your book is current with all your previous experience and that it represents all the different looks you can achieve. Many models work with professional photographers on test-shoots and even offer to model for photography students—a good source of free photos for your book. A positive, upbeat manner and a professional manner (showing up on time, taking direction well, not complaining about long hours or uncomfortable positions) are also very important. You want to show people that you are easy to work with. Models need to be photogenic and physically attractive, and need to meet certain height, weight, and body measurements required by the industry. Also useful is a familiarity with different modeling techniques and fashion show procedures, and experience with makeup and hairstyling.

Personal Stylist

Personal stylists work with individuals, groups, and companies to educate their clients about fashion apparel and accessories. Sometimes they give presentations or classes for small groups. They evaluate their client's physical attributes, lifestyles, careers, and fashion sense and make recommendations about which kinds of apparel and accessories will flatter them and help them attain their desired image. Sometimes they shop for their clients, choosing a sampling of items for that person to try on. Some stylists work for high-profile clients, such as actors, politicians, and athletes who want to project a certain image to the public.

A background in retail sales is excellent preparation for this job. There is no specific educational requirement for this position, but a college degree in fashion design or fashion merchandising can be very helpful. Personal stylists have an excellent eye for fashion and style, a thorough knowledge of fashion trends and forecasts, and enjoy shopping. Other useful traits include an outgoing personality and good communication skills.

Chapter 4

Tips for Success

Many of the keys to success in the fashion world are the same tools that a job seeker would be wise to employ in any field. As in most professions, who you know can make all the difference, and in this chapter you will find suggestions for effective networking that are specific to the fashion industry. To advance your career in a business so focused on appearance, you will need to pay special attention to the image you present on the job, how you dress for an interview and arrange your portfolio, and most important, how you are known in the workplace—your professional reputation.

Establishing Your Reputation

Many people who are initially attracted to the fashion industry for its glamour and prestige are in for a rude awakening. Most find out quickly that it is a tough, highly competitive business where people in low-level jobs are paid extremely poorly for the long hours they put in. Topping the list of complaints from employees in the industry is how low the starting salaries can be. If you already have your foot in the door, you probably know this only too well. Once you recover from the shock, however, you can start planning for your future in the industry and figure out the best strategies for moving into a better-paid position where your talents will shine. Following are some ways to make sure those long hours on the job work to your ultimate advantage. The following tips will help set you apart from your coworkers and help you advance in the fashion industry.

Demonstrate Your Flexibility

A "that is not in my job description" attitude will get you nowhere, especially in a tough job market. Show your employer that you are flexible and willing to assume additional responsibilities you did not originally sign up for. You may also be asked to take a temporary pay cut to help your company weather a rough economic patch. If you can do this cheerfully, you may be in a position to negotiate for a raise when times improve.

Take on Additional Duties

If you have some downtime on the job, make an effort to notice areas where coworkers may be struggling to meet deadlines or accomplish tasks and lend a hand in whatever ways that your current workload allows you to.

Check Your Ego at the Door

Dennis Gay, the onetime senior vice president and division head of Liz Claiborne Collection, once said, "If you work here you cannot have an ego. Your original ideas never go through unchanged. Everything is done by committee. It is a daily challenge to depersonalize yourself from the product and take a hard look at it and think, 'Is this what women in America want to buy?'"

Much of the work in fashion is achieved collaboratively, with many people working together to achieve the best possible result. If one of your pet ideas or projects is rejected in favor of something else, try not to take it personally and instead look at the big picture.

Whistle While You Work

You may be laboring like a dwarf in a diamond mine, but make sure you generate a positive attitude on the job. Keep your eyes on the prize, and remember that the long and often thankless hours you spend in low-paying, low-level fashion jobs are the necessary first steps for securing a better position down the line. You will get there even faster if people actually enjoy being around you. A little commiseration helps build relationships with employees in the same boat as you, especially if it is done in a humorous way. However, you definitely do not want to become known as a malcontent. (That said, you have rights as an employee to a safe and non-intimidating work environment. If one of your managers is clearly infringing on those rights—making inappropriate comments about your weight, for instance—you should report this to someone in human resources.)

Make Time to Volunteer

Philanthropy is an important element of the fashion industry, which has given rise to an entire field of "cause-related marketing." High-profile fund-raising efforts, such as the annual Heart Truth fashion show, when celebrities strut the stage in red dresses to promote awareness about the risks of heart disease for women, have become fixtures of the industry. High-profile industry figures spend lots of time socializing at these types of events, which generate plenty of publicity. As Kenneth Cole once said, "Philanthropy has been part of our corporate culture from the beginning." You can help distinguish yourself by volunteering for these types of charity and fund-raising events. Find a cause that is meaningful to you, and arrange to help out at a related event. By being there, you may make connections that prove helpful down the line, you will demonstrate to others that you are a generous and thoughtful person, and you will show people that you understand the role of philanthropy within the industry.

Getting Ahead

You may have heard the expression "glass ceiling." What that metaphor means is that a woman in business is only able to rise so far, and earn so much, in relation to a man in an equivalent position. In an industry such as the fashion business where women outnumber men (it is, in fact, the world's largest employer of women), one would assume that discrimination because of gender might not be the problem to the degree that it is in other traditionally male-dominated fields such as finance and advertising. Still, while women account for 52 percent of the workforce in the fashion and textiles industry, they occupy just 37 percent of the top jobs. In addition, many of the jobs in the industry are low-paying positions in apparel manufacturing and retail.

The workforce in this industry is an extremely diverse one, so people do not generally encounter a lot of discrimination on the basis of race and sexual orientation. Gay men, in particular, have a

Keeping
in Touch

Industry Contacts:
Meet Everyone You Can

Elizabeth Benator, who served as a fashion design career advisor at Parsons School of Design from 2003 until 2006, and who now recruits designers for her clients, advises people to never pass up the opportunity to have a conversation with someone in the business, even if you do not think it will lead anywhere. For instance, do not turn down the chance to interview for a position just because you are not really certain you want that particular job. If you make a positive impression on someone, they may recommend you to someone else. You never know what may come of it. In an industry where connections are everything, you should never turn down the chance to meet somebody new.

high visibility in the industry. That does not mean that the fashion business is one big, happy family, however. Competition is fierce, and not everyone follows the rules. Insiders will tell you there can be a lot of backstabbing in this business. The types of creative people that the industry tends to attract can be eccentric or have oversized egos and be difficult to work with. Following are some suggestions to help you rise to the top of this challenging field.

Edit Your Online Profile

What does your online profile say about you? If an employer Googled your name (and they do, frequently, to learn about an applicant), what would that person discover? Do you have photographs posted on your Facebook page that are immature, unprofessional, or perhaps even offensive? If so, you need to edit your profile or set it to "private." Do not give a potential employer any reason to eliminate you from the running for a job. A teacher caught one of her students bragging on her Facebook page about a term paper that she had plagiarized. You are smarter than that, aren't you?

Build Your Own Brand

To get ahead in the fashion industry, it can be useful to think of yourself as a brand. Create a distinctive look for the materials you use in your job search, such as your portfolio, business card, cover letter, and résumé. Choose the fonts, colors, layouts, and other design elements carefully and used them consistently.

Build Skills for a Global Industry

As more and more of the business moves overseas, foreign language skills (especially in languages such as French, Italian, Russian, Chinese, and Arabic) will help distinguish you in the workplace, so be sure you emphasize them on your résumé. If you do not speak another language, consider investing the time in learning one. Your local library will have language-learning program tapes you can borrow if you do not have the time or money to take a course, and a pair of headphones can put the time spent during a lengthy commute to good use. For similar reasons, a willingness to work overseas can be an asset. While it is true that many jobs in fashion have been outsourced, U.S. firms with overseas production plants in places like China and India still need supervisors and managers to oversee their operations.

Many jobs in the fashion industry require employees to travel—some of this may be by plane, and when you arrive at your destination you may be required to rent a car and drive to one or several destinations. If you do not have a driver's license, you will obviously need one for this type of work. But even if you are a licensed driver, unpaid parking tickets or a speeding ticket may result in points being taken off your license or even a suspension. In small businesses and sales jobs, a clean driving record is often required.

Find a Mentor

The word *mentor* goes back to Greek mythology. The goddess Athena transformed into the form of Mentor who gave advice to Odysseus. Nearly every person consulted in the course of researching this book stressed how invaluable mentors were in furthering their fashion careers. If you have been in the fashion industry a few years, you may have already identified a potential mentor in your place of employment or during an internship. You can try to network with someone you admire professionally, perhaps inviting that person out to lunch to ask them questions about their position. Once you identify a good mentoring candidate, keep these tips in mind:

→ **Schedule regular meetings.** Many begin mentorships with good intentions. They have an initial lunch and a few phone calls but then they get busy and the mentor relationship falls apart. However, if you schedule a regular meeting every four to six weeks, then it becomes a routine that can help you gain significant advice and direction.

→ **Come prepared.** Before you meet, know what you want to talk about. You might want to bring up some of your goals and ask for pointers on how you might reach them. You might ask your mentor for suggestions of books, conferences, workshops, professional organizations, and other resources that can give you a leg up in the industry.

→ **Do not be a pest.** Try to stick to your regular appointments with a mentor and do not be afraid to call occasionally with a specific question. But do not be too pushy or constantly in contact. Make sure your mentor has breathing room, and if they get busy, it is OK to skip the regular meeting now and then.

→ **Show respect.** Always remember that the mentor is giving his or her time to you. Make sure you are always on time to meetings. Be polite. Be attentive to all he or she says.

→ **Evaluate whether your mentorship is working.** After a few mentor meetings, take a step back and ask yourself if you are truly getting helpful advice, job leads, and information that is furthering your goals. If the mentorship is not working for you, you will have to be honest, end your relationship, and start looking for another. Like any relationship, a good mentor relationship can be a matter of chemistry and that can take some time to develop.

Network, Network, Network

The majority of jobs in fashion are found through personal relationships and connections. Join an organization in the fashion industry, accept any invitations that come your way, attend workshops and seminars, read trade magazines and fashion blogs, and talk to everybody you can in the business in person and via social networking sites like Facebook and LinkedIn. If you are a graduate of a fashion school, your school likely offers you access to alumni networks. Make use of them!

Work Traits That Lead to Success

These tips apply to any job, and you should follow them if you want to get ahead. You may already know these basics, but it is good to review them once in a while to make sure you are on track with these business fundamentals.

- ➡ **Always be on time.** Every employer values punctuality and many will not tolerate lateness. Be late a few times in a row and you may find yourself out of a job. By the same token, do not leave at 4:59 if the day ends at 5 p.m. Put in extra time until the work gets done. And do not take an extra long lunch.
- ➡ **Be eager to learn.** Employers value those who want to find out more about operations and chip in where needed.
- ➡ **Know you are being evaluated.** When you start a job, employers often consider the first few weeks a "probationary period." They will be keeping a close eye on you, your attitude, and performance. You should know the exact terms of this evaluation period.
- ➡ **Keep a neat desk.** A messy desk does not make a good impression. Do not keep soda cans on your desktop; do not store stinky gym shorts and shoes in your work area.
- ➡ **Get all your basic tools right away.** Find out if you need an office key or lock codes. You may need passwords for computers and codes for a copy machine as well. Make sure you have the basic office supplies you need for your job. You may need to be fill out specific forms as well. Some companies will require that you log your hours and keep careful track.
- ➡ **Know the rules and protocol.** Every business has its distinct rules of operation. Be sure you go over them with your boss or someone who works in human resources.
- ➡ **Take the initiative.** If you find yourself with nothing to do, ask your superior how you can help. Do not use downtime to goof off—answering personal e-mails, surfing the Web, and so on.

➡ **Take responsibility for mistakes.** We all goof up sometimes. When you do make a mistake, tell what the mistake is and suggest ways that it can be corrected.

➡ **Be ready for a performance review.** Most businesses give their employees a review at least once a year. Raises, bonuses, promotions, and simply continuing your employment depends on how you do in a review, so when yours comes up, be ready. Make a list of your accomplishments and how you have been contributing to the company. Take criticism well. Listen and ask for suggestions on how to improve or make your own suggestions. Take notes so you know what you should be doing to improve and what your boss expects in the months ahead.

➡ **Maintain workplace etiquette.** Do not be a gossip. Do not date someone you work with, no matter how tempting.

Designing Your Career Path

Some insiders will tell you that working your way up through the ranks of a single company is the only way to succeed in the fashion business. Other people insist that the only way to advance in the industry is to switch from one company or firm to another. Both avenues can be paths to success, as you will see.

Staying Put to Advance

Many large specialty chains, department stores, and mass merchandisers have a management training track that promotes employees from within. Executive (management) trainees may be interviewed for management track careers before they graduate from college. Retail managers carefully select individuals for these limited openings. They are looking for people who are serious about retailing as a career and who are willing to learn the business from the ground up. Management training programs typically last from between six months to two years. During this period, trainees receive instructions in areas such as supervising and motivating sales personnel, along with different techniques for sales, customer service, and merchandise classification, and presentation. They also learn about the store's different branches, selling departments, nonselling jobs, cost control, various promotional techniques, pricing, and time management, among other things. After completing this program, trainees usually choose one of two specific career tracks—either merchandise management or operations management—on the basis of their aptitudes and interests. If you are interested in the merchandise management branch of retailing, your career ladder would lead from assistant buyer, to buyer, to divisional merchandise manager (or DMM), to general merchandise manager (GMM), and finally to vice president of merchandising. If you opt for the operations management track, your career path will typically include the following jobs: assistant department manager, department manager, assistant store manager, store manager, district manager, regional manager, and finally vice president of operations.

Kevin Harter, the vice president of fashion direction at Bloomingdale's flagship store in New York, who provided the foreword for this book, started his career at Bloomingdale's in Chicago as a sales associate. A few months after starting in that position, Harter's bosses asked him to go into the management training program. Harter began rising through the ranks on the store line, or operations path, but then made a switch back to the merchandising track. Now he occupies the prestigious position of vice president of fashion direction for men's, home, and dot com, and says proudly, "I have pretty much spent my whole career at Bloomingdale's."

Evie Huntington (see interview on page 108) also moved up through the merchandising management ranks at Macy's, beginning as a buyer and ultimately working her way up to merchandising vice president. Large retailers like Bloomingdale's and Macy's are clearly invested in grooming employees for management positions, encouraging them to spend their careers with the same employer, and they do much of their hiring and promotions in-house. Other companies prefer to hire or recruit people from other companies, who can bring fresh perspectives and different backgrounds to the job.

Switching Companies to Move Up

Sue Goodwin's career path has taken her all over the world. Beginning as a designer in Dallas, Texas, she acquired skills in product development and production that helped her land a New York job with a leading designer of contemporary women's fashion. The business was a partnership with a Hong Kong factory, and Goodwin spent the next five years living and working in that city before returning to New York. Stints at Liz Claiborne, Dana Buchman, and Jones Apparel followed. She is currently the senior director for knitwear production at Ralph Lauren's Purple and Black Labels. Goodwin's willingness to relocate and to change jobs and companies allowed her to take advantage of the opportunities that came her way.

Making a Career Change into Fashion

If you have no previous fashion experience and are contemplating a career move into the fashion industry, a graduate program may be a wise choice. Many schools with fashion programs, such as FIT, also offer graduate programs.

Greta Earnest, the assistant director of the library at FIT (see interview page 14), initially trained as a teenager at the world's most prestigious fashion academy, the Chambre Syndicale de la Couture Parisienne, but then decided to change course. She got her undergraduate degree in art history and eventually earned a graduate degree in library science. After working for 20 years in the fields of art and architecture, Earnest decided to return to her fashion roots when she took a job at FIT. She was able to bring all those various elements of her background to her current position.

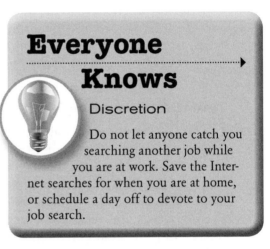

Everyone Knows

Discretion

Do not let anyone catch you searching another job while you are at work. Save the Internet searches for when you are at home, or schedule a day off to devote to your job search.

Few continuing education courses exist for those already working in the industry, though some schools—such as Parsons—do offer them. Online classes are another option. You can add to your knowledge by attending trade shows and seminars thrown by industry groups to help people employed in fashion to keep up with trends and developments in the industry.

Advice for the Job Hunt

Thoroughly research the options in your geographical area before you begin your job hunt. A well-informed applicant is always preferable to one who has not taken the time to study the trends and workings of the market.

Where the Jobs Are

According to the experts, 75 percent of job in the fashion industry are found through networking, so that is where you should concentrate most of your efforts. If you are a fashion school graduate, the first place you should contact is the alumni services department of the school you attended. The success of an institution is gauged, in part, by the percentage of graduates they place in the industry, so schools are very invested in helping graduate find jobs. Your alma mater can help you network with other alumni and sometimes help you find a mentor in the industry.

While not as effective as networking, the classifieds, newspapers, and the Internet are also important avenues for your job search. Trade papers such as *Women's Wear Daily* include job lists, as do Internet job boards such as Vault.com and Stylecareers.com.

Timing Is Everything

The fashion business is traditionally organized around designers' spring/summer and fall/winter collections, shown during "fashion weeks" on the runways months ahead of time. Spring collections are typically shown between September and November, and the fall/winter collections are showcased from January through March. Fashion weeks are week-long events held in the "big four" fashion capitals of New York, London, Milan, and Paris (in that order), as well as in many other cities around the world. There are also genre-specific fashion weeks for items such as swimwear bridal collections. Such events allow industry insiders—including members of the fashion press, other designers, celebrities, and buyers—to preview the designs for the coming season. Fashion trade shows are also scheduled at the same time each year, usually in the same cities. If you are trying to connect with someone, you can access online fashion calendars (see fashioncalendar.net, or fashionindustrycalendar.com, for instance) to see when people will and will not be available, when their busiest times will be, and plan your approach accordingly. For instance, if you are working in the women's wear industry and you are planning a career move into menswear, you should know that the busiest times in that industry are the Milan fashion weeks, where the menswear collections are shown, and the annual MAGIC trade show in Las Vegas that takes place at the end of August and beginning of September. Do not try to schedule an interview during those times. You will increase your chances of making contact as well as demonstrate your understanding of the industry if you choose to approach people at a time when they will not be busy attending or preparing for any major industry events.

Identify Potential Growth Areas in the Industry

While a significant portion of fashion jobs have moved overseas, there are still many areas where forecasters are expecting to see growth during the next decade. Focus your job hunt in areas that have the potential for growth.

As of 2009, industry insiders were predicting there will be growth in the areas of outerwear, high-tech performance fabrics, and private label clothing and accessories. Technology fashion accessories such as cell-phone covers and laptop cases are also becoming very popular. The average size of people in the United States, and increasingly in westernized countries overseas, is growing, which means that the demand for stylish plus-size clothing (sizes 14–28) has also grown. An increasing trend toward customization and personalization of apparel and the shopping experience will likely create new opportunities in the industry as well. Body scanning technology can used to help customize fit, enabling a garment to be digitally tailored to a specific customer's measurements. Programs such as The Digital Dressing Room allow customers to input their own images and then virtually "try on" apparel in cyberspace. Customers seeking more personalized apparel can request that a particular item, such as an athletic shoe, be produced in a particular color with a particular motif. Advances in radio frequency identification (RFID) technology have been used in retailing to further customize the shopping experience. When a customer brings a piece of clothing into the dressing room, an RFID reader can provide suggestions of which garments and accessories would complement that item.

Today, menswear is approximately 24 percent of the apparel market and is undergoing some exciting changes. In 2009, following a generally difficult year in the apparel industry, Bloomingdale's flagship store in New York unveiled its brand-new three-story, 90,000 square-foot men's store. Fashion insiders such as Kevin Harter (see Foreword) are convinced that more men today are fashion conscious and informed about style and shopping for themselves, rather than letting the women in their lives shop for them. Stay informed about ongoing developments in the industry. Changing times create new opportunities for the job seeker.

Interviewing for a Fashion Job

Fashion is a unique and singular industry—something apparent even in the unspoken protocol of its job interviews.

Dressing the Part

In the fashion industry, appearance counts for more than it does in many other industries. On TLC's long-running makeover show *What Not to Wear*, Clinton Kelly and Stacy London offer some sound advice for anyone seeking to launch their career: Dress for the job you want, not for the job you have.

Given that this is the fashion industry, how you look and dress will definitely make an impression. People applying for creative jobs such as stylists and designers, as well as sales associates who work directly with the public, will want to pay special attention to this, since they have an opportunity to convey a lot about their own fashion sense and style in the pieces they choose to wear to an interview. The outfit that you wear will also show whether you would be a good fit within the culture of the company where you are applying and that you understand what they are all about. So, select your clothing and your accessories with great care. Do not overdo it, however. If you are a designer, you may certainly wear one of your own creations, but it should be appropriate for the occasion. (If you design swimsuits, do not wear a bikini!) If you are not entirely sure about the dress code at a company where you are applying, it is better to err on the side of being a little overdressed. And bear in mind that the majority of people who work in fashion are not gorgeous, skinny, young women dressed in Manolo Blahnik shoes and couture clothes. Here are some ways to make sure you are appropriately dressed for an interview:

➜ **Thoroughly research the company where you are applying.** This can mean visiting their Web site or even shopping at one of their stores. Get a feeling for the company's overall style and the types of customers it attracts. If you know someone who has worked for that company, ask them to tell you about how people dress at work. When possible, arriving at an interview wearing a piece with the label of company where you are applying can be a good move. If you cannot afford their apparel, you may be able to find a vintage piece.

➧ **Always be neat, even if the company where you are applying has a very casual style.** If you are applying for a position at a Rock & Republic, for example, it may be appropriate to wear jeans to an interview, but be sure they have a dark wash and look crisp. If you are planning to wear sandals, consider getting a pedicure.

➧ **Make sure that you will be comfortable in whatever you are intending to wear.** You will want to devote all of your attention to the person interviewing you and not have to worry about shoes that pinch or a too-tight waistband.

➧ **Do not show too much skin.** Cover up that cleavage and opt for skirts or dresses that hit just above the knee or below. No short shorts or micro-minis, even if the company you are applying to specializes in those items.

➧ **Female job applicants should play it safe and wear sheer black hose or opaque tights if they are wearing a skirt or dress.** Bare legs may be acceptable at the company you are applying for, but it is best not to make that assumption.

Making Your Portfolio Work for You

Your portfolio is the most powerful self-marketing tool you have, so it is worth investing the time and money into making it as effective as it can be. Jobs that require a portfolio include fashion designer, graphic designer, fashion illustrator, fashion photographer, and other creative positions in the industry. Give plenty of thought to how you arrange the selections in your portfolio. Select 15 to 20 pieces of your best work to include, and make high-resolution scans to include in the portfolio. (Do not include original work, since it may get damaged or lost.) Remove any examples of work that do not directly relate to the job you are seeking. Edit your portfolio carefully to demonstrate how suited you are to work at the specific company where you are applying. As designer Karl Aberg says, "If you are interviewing at Polo, your portfolio shouldn't look like Versace!" The running order of artwork needs to flow smoothly—you want to encourage the viewer to keep turning pages. Orient all pieces the same way so the viewer does not have the turn the book to view anything. You can choose to group your work chronologically to show development, or according to themes and styles, but whatever system you choose should be clear and logical for the viewer. Put your best pieces at the start and the end—these are often known as conversation pieces, because ideally they will be pieces the viewer will want to discuss further. Only include work that you feel comfortable discussing—if you have any pieces you are not entirely happy with, leave them out. Make an effort to include pieces that demonstrate your creativity as well as some that could fit right in on their sales floor. If possible, include a group that is geared toward the season they are working on now. Designers usually work a year in advance, so if you are interviewing in October of 2010, they are probably putting together their Fall 2011 collection.

Make sure your portfolio is clearly labeled with your name and contact information, and be sure to include a few copies of your résumé. Do not leave your portfolio behind to be looked at later by someone who is absent. Always make another appointment to return with your portfolio in hand for that person to review. Not all companies or individuals are honest, and you do not want to give anyone the chance to appropriate the work that you have labored so hard on.

You should always save your work digitally, too. Scan the artwork at high resolution and save it onto a disk. Save digital files in a JPEG or PDF format, and keep the file size per image on the small side (300 to 500 kb). You can e-mail a digital file to potential employers, but be sure to check first to see which form they would prefer to review the work in. Make sure to label all digital files carefully, with your last name, first name, and a brief description of what you are sending. Many professionals have their own Web site on which they include the artwork in their portfolios and to which they can refer potential employers.

General Interviewing Tips

The fashion industry has its own distinct culture and requirements. However, much of the advice that career counselors give to people applying for jobs in other industries can apply to fashion, too. As the old saying goes, first impressions really do count. Studies have shown that people form impressions within the first seven seconds of meeting someone, and that most of these impressions are based on visual information and nonverbal cues. The job interview is your chance to make a good first impression. If you have not been on a job interview in a while, some of these tips can help you when you go in to meet face-to-face with the person who can hire you. Some of these may seem like no-brainers, but people who work in human resources can tell you plenty of horror stories about clueless people who apply for jobs wearing ear buds, or who stop to answer their cell phones in the middle of an interview. Read on for some advice that can help you ace your interview:

→ **Know the details about the position.** When you find out about a job opening, find out as much as you can about the job ahead of time so you can explain how your interests and qualifications match the job description. If you have questions about the position ahead of time, you may be able to clarify information by phone, speaking to someone in human resources, a receptionist, or another person on staff. You want to be as ready as possible to explain how your talents fit the job.

→ **Do your homework. Research the establishment that is offering a position.** Find out its history, achievement, and plans for the future. This can help you develop intelligent questions to ask during the interview and make it easier to explain how you can contribute.

→ **Arrive on time.** There is no such thing as being "fashionably late" to a job interview. Punctuality is one of the biggest factors to making a good first impression. If you arrive late to an interview, it is a strike against you and can cost you getting a job. Every employer wants to hire people who are on time. Always be on the safe side and arrive 10 minutes early.

→ **Do not chew gum.**

→ **Avoid making jokes or using slang or profanity.** A little humor is OK and can set everyone at ease, but you never want to give the impression that you are not a serious candidate for the position.

→ **Turn off that cell phone!**

→ **Come prepared.** Make sure you have everything with you that you will need. Ask if you should bring a copy of your résumé, a list of references, or a transcript of grades, if required. Check if the employer wants to see samples of your work. For a creative position, you will be expected to bring a portfolio (see above) demonstrating the range of your work.

➜ **Talk about background that relates to the job.** The fashion industry is a very creative field and very creative people work in it, so you can bring up aspects of your past that demonstrate your interest in fashion and style.

➜ **Be ready for some standard questions.** Most interviews cover the same territory and familiar questions. Some of the standards are:

- *Tell me about yourself.* This is where you go back over your education and applicable job history and mention your professional goals and why you are there in the first place.

- *What's your biggest weakness?* This one comes up often enough and can trip up the interviewee. It might be wise to redirect the question and talk about what was a weakness for you and how you have been working to improve yourself in a particular area. For example, you might say you were not totally familiar with Adobe Illustrator software, but you have been taking time each week to master it.

- *What salary are you looking for?* Salary negotiation is always tricky. You do not want to undervalue yourself and you do not want to price yourself out of a job. Emphasize that you applied because you are interested in the job. That is your first priority and you can come to salary terms once you determine if you are right for the position.

- *Why should I hire you?* You have to turn on the charm and say how you can really contribute to the company and stress the qualifications that make you the ideal candidate.

➜ **Ask questions.** If you have done your research on the company, you will be able to ask intelligent questions about your employer that show you have a true interest in their operations. You can do plenty of research by checking the employer's Web site and searching for information on the Internet. Smart inquiries about the company's history, products, services, and future goals shows that you are enthusiastic and want to be a part of operations.

➜ **Be positive.** Positive attitude goes a long way in any business, so be as upbeat as possible.

→ **Be willing to start small.** If you are trying to enter the fashion industry with little experience, expect to take a position with little responsibility, low pay, and a lot of grunt work. Once you get a foot in the door, you can learn more about the business, prove yourself, and advance.

→ **Ask for a business card at the end of the interview.** You will need to know the correct spelling of names, titles, and e-mail addresses to follow up with the person you spoke to.

Problem
Solving

A Tale of Two Blouses

Margot works as a salesperson at an exclusive boutique. One day, she is approached by a frequent customer who wants to return a blouse, claiming she changed her mind about it when she got home. When Margot examines the garment, however, it is clear that it has been worn—perhaps repeatedly. Margot does not want to lose a good customer, but she has reason to doubt the woman's story. What should Margot do?

Unlike larger retailers who can take back returns without question, Margot's employer cannot afford a "no questions asked" return policy, which is why she posts a sign saying "Store Credit Only" next to the cash register. She also cannot sell merchandise that shows signs of wear. Margot has to refuse the customer's request and point out the evidence: soil around the collar and traces of deodorant under the arms. However, Margot makes certain that she remains pleasant and businesslike when she delivers the bad news, and she allows the customer a chance to explain. As it turns out, the customer had purchased two similar blouses and mistakenly grabbed the wrong one on her way to the shop. She returns the following day with the correct garment, and Margot gives her credit for the full purchase amount.

Some people try to take advantage of retailers in various ways, and Margot was right to be wary. However, this was a simple mistake. By remaining pleasant, treating the woman with respect, and giving her the benefit of the doubt, Margot helped her boss to retain a loyal customer.

➜ **Send a follow-up thank-you note.** Do not under-estimate the power of the follow-up thank-you note. Send one out very soon after the interview to show how prompt and efficient you are. Thank the interviewer for her or his consideration and again emphasize how much you want the job. Even if you are not interested in the job, it is crucial that you write to thank the interviewer for his or her time, and return any phone calls you may subsequently receive from that employer.

Professional
Ethics

Copyright Concerns

Competition in the fashion business can be fierce. Alex, an aspiring designer, found that out the hard way. The apparel company where he had recently been hired planned to start a new line of maternity clothes for stylish moms and announced, in house, that it was looking for a hip, new designer to develop a prototype collection. Alex spent hours at home sketching, putting together a collection of looks, along with fabric samples. An assistant designer in another department, Nina, and Alex got to talking, and Alex showed Nina a few of his designs and asked for some feedback. The following week, Alex was startled when a company memo went out announcing that Nina had been selected to design the new maternity line. Alex saw that the promotional materials for the new line featured some designs that closely resembled those he showed Nina. If Alex confronted Nina about it, she would likely deny any wrongdoing. Alex also worried that if he went to his boss with his complaints, it would seem like a case of sour grapes and only make him look like a troublemaker.

This is a tough situation, since designs cannot be copyrighted. Designers frequently draw their inspiration from other designers, though not always so blatantly. Nina should have been up front with Alex about her own interest in the position, but she had a right to apply for the job, too. Although he was angry, Alex decided it was in his best interest to look for another opportunity to distinguish himself within the company in a positive way. He has since learned to be a lot more cautious about whom he shares his ideas with.

Résumé Advice

A résumé is still an essential tool for showing your work experience and education. Formats can vary, but certain aspects of résumés are universal. It may just be a page or two, but your résumé has to give a concise snapshot of your work history and help convince an employer that you are the right person for the job.

➜ **You do not have to include every job you ever had.** You should feature the experience that best applies for the work you are seeking and you usually do not have to show your early jobs as a newspaper carrier or babysitter. Some jobs you held may be completely irrelevant, so you should leave them off.

➜ **Emphasize skills that apply to the job.** Each job is unique, but you will want to stress the skills needed for a specific position. The more varied projects you list, the better. It shows you have diverse skills and can juggle different projects.

➜ **Stress applicable knowledge in the education section.** Every résumé will list an applicant's higher education credentials. If you were involved in applicable extracurricular activities, such as working at a local fashion show benefit, you might mention that fact here. You may also list honors and awards.

➜ **Do not leave out intern or volunteer experience.** Even if you did not get paid at a job, if you learned pertinent skills, you will want to list those experiences and the talents you developed.

➜ **Include activities and interests.** Résumés typically have interesting items about an applicant's life because they can serve as a "hook," something that intrigues the reader and can be the basis for conversation. You may collect Bakelite jewelry or own a pet iguana. If there is an unusual aspect of your life worth sharing, it can pique interest and conversation in an interview.

➜ **Know how to submit your résumé online.** Nowadays, most employers will ask you to send in your résumé electronically, attached to an e-mail as a Microsoft Word document. Be sure to label your résumé document so it can be quickly identified: [your last name] résumé for [name of position].

→ **Customize your résumé.** You can create different versions of your résumé, depending on which position you are seeking or which company you are applying at. You can modify the information to emphasize different aspects of your work history or background.

→ **Keep your résumé up to date.** You may not have been on the job market for a while, but you need to make sure that your résumé reflects all the experience and responsibilities you have gained on the job. Keep track of which version you send to an employer.

→ **Avoid using Times New Roman.** This font is most commonly used in corporate résumé design and may suggest to your reader that you lack imagination. Opt instead for an interesting, legible font such as Arial, Century Gothic, Garamond, or Helvetica. Do not use more than two typefaces, however, or your résumé may look overdesigned.

→ **Pay a proofreader.** What is the big deal about a little typo? Your career could hinge on it—that is all. Make absolutely sure that your résumé is error-free, because that single mistake may be enough to eliminate you from the running, regardless of the position for which you are applying. Functions such as Spellcheck on your computer are notorious for all the errors they miss. Be sure you have someone skilled proofread your résumé for typos and other errors, even if you have to pay them.

Crafting a Winning Cover Letter

Whether sending in a hard copy résumé or an e-mailed one, you will need to write a cover note or letter to go along with it. This is your opportunity to show you have strong communication skills and can write in a professional manner. Avoid using contractions, abbreviations, and slang. You will need to proofread your letter carefully to catch any typos, misspellings, and grammatical mistakes. As with your résumé, you may even want to hire someone, or ask a trustworthy friend, to proofread it for you. Double check that you have changed the company names and addresses for every cover letter that you send.

The cover letter is your chance to give the reader a quick sense of who you are as a person. You might convey that you are a serious worker but you have a positive attitude and a sense of humor. In the letter, you should identify the job you are applying for and possibly mention how you heard about the position. Introduce yourself and give a sense of the experience you have that makes you right for the position. Explain why the company should be interested in you. For instance, you have been writing a fashion blog for several years that has generated a lot of interest in the industry, or your current job at an art gallery helping to hang shows has given you ideas about how best to light and display accessories in effective ways. All you need is an introduction, one to three paragraphs of text, and a short wrap-up paragraph suggesting the next course of action (for example, "I will contact you in a few days to follow up"). You may impress your reader by showing you have done some research on the organization. If you are entering the field with little direct experience, you will have to stress your applicable and transferable skills and highlight why you would still be right the position. Even though your contact information should be on your résumé, make sure it is on your cover letter as well as a precaution.

The best way to get accurate contact information for a company is to call them directly and ask for the human resources department. Be sure that the person you speak to spells out the name and official title of the person to whom you will be directing your letter.

References and Letters of Recommendation

If an employer is seriously considering you as a job candidate, he or she will want to contact references and perhaps see letters of recommendation. Generally, you need three to five references—people who are willing to endorse you as a worker and can speak about your prior experience. You usually present your references on a prepared list that is not your résumé. The list needs to include reference names, title, and contact information. Remember, these should be professionals who can vouch for your professionalism, so do not list friends and family members. Be sure that your references know that they are your references. Tell them what jobs you are applying for and that they might be contacted by an employer. You can coach the reference in advance as well. If you are applying for a sales position, tell your reference to play up your communication skills and any related experience.

INTERVIEW

On the Fast Track

Evie Huntington
President, Evie Huntington and Associates, Seattle, Washington

What is your official title, and what exactly do you do?
I am a staffing and recruiting consultant for the retail wholesale industry, and I specialize in the Pacific Northwest.

**What was your preparation to work in this position? Please
describe what your career path was like.**
I attended parochial school through high school and wore a uniform
and was dying to get into the fashion industry and become a buyer. So
I joined a fashion board my senior year in high school and proceeded
to work my way through college on the sales floor of a small specialty
retailer in Seattle. When I graduated I joined the Bon Marché, which
is now Macy's, got into their training program, and was a buyer in 11
months. I spent another 20 years and worked my way up to a merchandising vice president. So I started out as a buyer and then worked
my way up to supervising a staff of 14—seven buyers and their assistants. In the mid-nineties I wanted to make a career switch—staying
in the industry but no longer traveling. I wanted to move into an HR
role because I spent a lot of years mentoring and training young buying associates and I had the opportunity to join Eddie Bauer in their
new recruiting division, and then within a few years I was the director of recruiting at Eddie Bauer. I left Eddie Bauer a few years ago to
start up my own company, Evie Huntington and Associates, and that
allowed me to spend more time traveling with my husband who's an
international business consultant. I now have my own recruiting business, and I've been doing that for about five years.

It sounds like you covered a lot of ground in that time.
I was very fortunate with regards to the people who mentored me
and brought me along. I had great people that supported me—from
presidents of the companies who put me under their wings and gave
me all the opportunities to grow and rise. I will say that I do not think
it is as fast now in this day and age as it was 25 years ago. I think that
is the difference. But I will admit that I was very fortunate and I was
fast-tracked—definitely fast-tracked. I was a buyer for four years and
a merchandise manager for about five years and I was a merchandis-

ing VP. But it was due to a very strong group of mentors that I had, not only in the merchandising side of the business but in the human resources side.

How did all the jobs that you had before you started your own business inform the work that you are doing now?
I think the key thing is that I had sales floor experience, store management experience, and then moved into the buying offices and worked my way up through the buying offices. Having that broad range of practical experience provided me with instant credibility when I moved into recruiting. I'd worked in all parts of the business and I'd worked as a buyer with all the manufacturers, so I had a pretty good understanding of the wholesale side of the business as well as the design and manufacturing side. My background in the industry provided me with the experience to be able to move into recruiting.

Did you set your sights on a recruiting position from the beginning?
Not at all. I always thought I was going to be president of the Bon Marché in the Pacific Northwest. But as time went by I realized that I was not interested in the traveling anymore. With this industry it is kind of addictive, meaning it is a very fast-paced industry and you are constantly moving and thinking ahead and working 6 to 18 months out, and you cannot really scale back. So I knew that I wanted to stay in the industry but I did not want to have to do extensive traveling, because we were on the road maybe one to two weeks a month on occasion.

What do you like best about your job and what is the most difficult part?
The greatest part for me now is that I am able to give back to people who gave so much to me, meaning that I can work with people and help foster their careers—make them consider other opportunities that maybe they haven't considered before, and offer advice. Career consulting is one of the things I do as well. I really enjoy working with people and finding the right fit for them and helping them grow and move in the direction they want to move in. So that is the most rewarding part of the business for me now.

I know the people that I am working with and I know the people that I am presenting as candidates to companies, so I think the biggest concern for me would be if I did not feel that a candidate was right for the company. However, since I know everybody fairly well I do not

(continues on next page)

INTERVIEW

On the Fast Track (continued)

have that issue. That is why I've structured my business to only recruit for the Pacific Northwest, because I want to believe in the company that I am recruiting for and I want to have confidence that the candidate I am presenting is a very viable candidate. I think the biggest frustration for other recruiters is if they are doing national recruiting, they do not have an intimate knowledge of the company and the company's politics and the environment that they are presenting candidates into, and they do not know the candidate they are presenting thoroughly and feel really comfortable with that fit.

So you are a really great matchmaker, it sounds like. Has it ever happened that a particular match did not work out?
I had one of those where we thought we'd really identified a candidate that we thought not only had the skill set but the desire to go into [fabric consulting], and be more in that side of business. But she worked much better in a much larger environment, a corporate environment, and did not do well in a smaller, more boutiquey-type business. So, yes, it does happen. And at that point in time there is no fee, and we go and start the search over again.

Are you working with people who are just entering the fashion industry or are you placing people higher up?
I work at the executive level mostly. So I work with directors, divisional merchandise managers, vice presidents, and senior vice presidents. I do not work at the CEO level, but senior management, absolutely. And I do a little bit of consulting, so I cover all bases.

How have evolving technologies impacted your job? How do you use technology in your work?
All of those sites—Facebook, LinkedIn, Monster—all of those technologies that allow you to be so connected throughout the industry so that you can source through that database. From a recruiting standpoint, it is like being in hog heaven! There are so many resources for you to go out and find the right people, and it did not used to be that way. If I am working for somebody and they say, "I want somebody

from Banana Republic for this position," I can go into the Internet and I can find those people. It used to be that companies would put up their firewalls—and you just had no way of sourcing into those companies. Now you can figure it out and you can get in, and it is fabulous. But it can also be overwhelming. When you post a job and you get 300 applicants it can be overwhelming—and for many companies it is overwhelming. It is hard to respond to all the applicants and there's so much frustration on the applicant's side because they say, "I am not hearing back from this company." That is what I do when I am counseling people. Everybody wants to work for the Bill and Melinda Gates Foundation, for instance, and I have to look at people and say, "You are not going to get a job there. They get over 3,000 applications a day, and you are going up against Harvard, Oxford, all the best talent in the entire world. And you do not bring any talents to the table other than the fact that you have a desire to work there." That is when I have to say, "You are never going to hear back from them, you are never going to get a job there." So that is the greatest frustration—people apply for jobs that they are not qualified for and it is really hard for recruiters to deal with that. It is just mountains and mountains of paper to go through.

Where do you think there might be growth in the industry in the next five years?
I do think that green jobs is a new, burgeoning part of the industry. Apparel manufacturers are going after products that are environmentally friendly because that is what the consumer wants to buy, and that is a whole new niche. But the other side to that is that now the consumer is going to have to pay more for this merchandise, and so they have to be prepared to pay more. They are also going to have to look at whatever they are buying and say, OK, I am paying more for it so it is going to have to last longer. It is not going to be disposable like it is been in the past. One of the things they are saying on the news now is wear your clothes longer, wear them out, do not be recycling them as quickly as they have. So the way people view fashion is going to change, because it is going to be about quality and not quantity, and they'll probably be paying more for it and keeping it longer. I volunteer at a place called St. Francis House that takes in apparel and we redistribute it to the homeless, and their donations are way down this year, because people are hanging on to their stuff. Companies are going to have to start providing a different type of product that is going to last longer, wear longer, and people will pay more for that. Again, that whole green side of the industry is going to be huge. I think the

(continues on next page)

INTERVIEW

On the Fast Track (continued)

younger generation is totally in tune with that, and that they'll be willing to spend the additional money and look at it as social responsibility.

On the basis of your own experience, what advice would you give to someone starting out in fashion? What do you wish someone had told you when you were just starting out?
I have a lot of practical experience, I worked on the sales floor through college, I went into store management and then moved into the buying training program, etc. I had a degree in history and a minor in English, but really it is a business, fashion is a business—it is not a passion, it is a business. I'd had some business classes, of which I had none, I would have been far better prepared to move in to the areas of responsibility that I did move in to as a buyer and as a merchandise manager and as a vice president. I had to get all of that learning on the job, and it took me longer to get up to speed where I was really effective and impactful. If you are going to go into this business you have to understand that it is a business. So you need to have a little of both. If you can take any merchandising or marketing classes, they are good to have. I am a big proponent of practical experience but if you can come with some schooling as well that will be very helpful.

Chapter 5

Talk Like a Pro

Knowing the vocabulary of the industry is an essential component to acquiring a position and getting ahead. Become familiar with the terms listed in this glossary. Consult it whenever you hear a word in conversation with other professionals that you do not understand.

accessories Articles worn or carried to complete a fashion look, such as jewelry, scarves, hats, handbags, and shoes.

acrylic A manufactured fiber derived from polyacrylonitrile. Its properties include a soft, wool-like hand, machine washable and dryable, and excellent color retention.

adaptation A design that reflects the outstanding features of another design but is not an exact copy.

add-ons Additional merchandise items, such as related items to create complete outfits.

advance buying Retail ordering of merchandise well ahead of the desired shipment date, usually at a lower price.

advance orders Merchandise orders with a longer lead time before the delivery date.

advertising Any paid form of nonpersonal sales message made by an identified sponsor through a mass communication medium.

advertising agencies Service firms that provide advertising expertise and design, produce, and place ads in the media.

alta moda The high fashion (couture) design industry of Italy.

alterations Changes to existing items.

anchor stores Major chain and department stores that provide the attraction needed to draw customers to shopping centers or malls, "destination stores."

apparel Clothing.

apparel industry The manufacturers, jobbers, and contractors engaged in the manufacture of clothing (also called the garment business, the needle trades, the rag trade).

apparel jobbers Outside shops that never produce any of their own goods.

apparel marts Buildings or complexes that house permanent showrooms of apparel manufacturers.

applied design Surface design added to fabric.

apprenticeship Training for an occupation by working under the direction and guidance of a skilled worker.

approval buying An arrangement in which merchandise is shipped to the retailer's store for inspection before the final purchase decision is made.

as ready Term denoting that a manufacturer promises to ship orders when they are completed rather than by an exact date.

artisans People who do skilled work with their hands.

assorters Also called assemblers, assorters are apparel manufacturing employees who prepare cut garment parts for production sewing.

assortment Diversification of goods, range of stock, or total selection offered.

atelier (ah-tel-YAY) French word for a designer workshop. Ateliers are classified as *flou* (for soft dressmaking) or *tailleur* (for tailoring suits and coats).

back orders Merchandise orders that have not been filled within the time specified and have not been canceled by the buyer.

backward integration Combining a business at one step of the distribution channel with another toward the beginning of the chain closer to the raw materials.

bagging Putting merchandise into a sack for better handling, protection, and privacy of customer purchases.

balance of trade The relationship between the values of a country's imports and exports, described as being a deficit of a surplus.

bar codes Standardized symbologies used on merchandise tags for electronic identification and collection of product data.

base goods The solid fabric used as the basis for a group of softwear.

bast fiber   Any of certain strong, woody fibers used in making rope, matting, or fabric.

bespoke   English term for made-to-measure men's suits.

bias grain   Diagonal grain of fabric.

blanket orders   Promises to buy from favored vendors over a period of time, with no detail of colors, sizes, or shipment until later.

bleaching   Chemical process that removes color, impurities, or spots from fibers or fabrics during fabric finishing or garment laundering.

blend   Yarn made by spinning together two or more different fibers, usually in staple form.

body scanning   A procedure to collect individual sizing information electronically.

boucle   A knit or woven fabric made from a rough, curly, knotted boucle yarn. The fabric has a looped, knotted surface and is often used in sportswear and coats.

boutique   French word for a small shop with unusual clothing and atmosphere; small stand-alone shops or distinctive areas within a larger store that sell unusual, few-of-a-kind apparel, accessories, or decorative items.

boys' sizes   Clothing sized 8 to 22 for boys in grade school through adolescence.

branch coordinator   Employee of a large retail organization who keep tabs on all the branches to see that their stock, selling techniques, and general operations coordinate with the main store or headquarters' policies.

branch store   A store owned and operated by a parent store; generally located in a suburban area under the name of the store or in metropolitan shopping areas.

brand   A name, label, or mark assigned to a product by its manufacturer.

brick and click   Industry buzz word to describe retail stores that have Web sites.

bridge lines   Secondary or "diffusion" lines of well-known designers priced between the designer and better categories.

bridge market   Clothing whose price points and styling fall between the designer and better market.

business casual   A popular dress code that emerged in white-collar workplaces during the 1970s. May mean quite different things in different companies and areas of the United States. In general, for men this means a sports coat in a muted color, cotton trousers with a belt, and a collared shirt with no tie. For women it usually means pantsuits, tailored pants, with a top or sweater set. Jeans and gym shoes are usually unacceptable for either gender.

business cycle Fluctuations in the level of economic activity that occur with some regularity over a period of time.

business ethics The use of good moral values in business dealings.

buyer A merchandising executive responsible for planning, buying, and selling merchandise.

buying office An independent or store-owned office that is located at a market center and buys for one chain or for many stores.

buying plan A plan that describes the types and quantities of merchandise to purchase for a department or store for a specific time period and for a set amount of money.

cashmere A luxury fiber obtained from the soft fleecy undergrowth of the Kashmir goat of Tibet, Mongolia, China, Iran, Iraq, and India. Most commonly used in sweaters, shawls, suits, coats, and dresses.

Everyone Knows

French Pronunciation

Many of the terms you will hear in the fashion industry are French, or derived from the French, because Paris has been the world's fashion capital for so long. Furthermore, many top designers' names—such as Hermès (AIR-mehz), Givenchy (Zshee-VON-she), and Comme des Garçons (Comb day gar-SON)—may be challenging to pronounce, or the pronunciations may not be immediately clear to you based on how they are spelled. You can save yourself a heap of embarrassment by making absolutely certain you know how to pronounce a term or a name before you speak it. And if you are not sure how to pronounce it, do not use it. Besides the dictionary, a good source for pronunciations can be found at http://hypebeast/2008/07/how-to-pronounce-designer-names-tutorial.

catalog showrooms   Stores that display sample items of merchandise mainly sold through catalogs.

category killers   Large discount specialty chains that carry huge selections of merchandise in a single product category at such low prices that they destroy the competition in their specialty area. Examples include The Sports Authority and Toys "R" Us.

caution   Admission or entrance fee required by haute couture houses from commercial customers to attend showings. It is intended to deter copying and is applied toward purchases.

chain stores   A group of stores (usually twelve or more) that is owned, managed, merchandised, and controlled by a central office.

Chambre Syndicale   Trade association for top designers of the Paris couture.

channel of distribution   The route that goods and services take from the original source through all middle people to the ultimate user.

checker   Commercial pattern company employee who sees that cutting and sewing markings are properly included and aligned.

chemical finishes   Finishes that become part of the fabrics through chemical reactions with the fibers.

cherry picking   Buyers' practice of selecting only a few items from each vendor that best represent their lines.

children's apparel   Clothing for girls ages 3–13 and boys ages 3–16.

children's sizes   Apparel sizes for preschoolers who are taller and more slender than toddlers.

classic   A fashion that is long-lasting; a style or design that continues to be popular over an extended period of time, even though fashions change.

classification buyers   Retail employees who plan, choose, purchase, price, and promote one classification of goods for all the stores in a chain or large store organization.

classification buying   Activity of purchasing only one category classification of merchandise, often done by chain store buyers. Also called central buying.

clearance merchandise   Low-priced promotional goods, usually featured in off-price discount stores or as sale items.

client book   A salesperson's book of customer's names, phone numbers and e-mail addresses, sizes, and important dates.

clienteling   The use of retail databases to identify individual retailers' most profitable shoppers.

closeout goods Selected discontinued goods, usually of various sizes and colors, sold at a low price.

closing the sale Getting a commitment from the customer to buy the merchandise.

closures Items used to close openings in apparel and other consumer textile products, such as buttons, buckles, snaps, zippers, and hook and eye.

code of ethics A written statement that sets forth the legal principles that should guide that organization's decisions.

collection The total number of garments in a designer's or apparel manufacturer's seasonal presentation, especially for high-priced garments.

colorfast Term designating that the color in a fabric will not face or change with laundering, dry cleaning, or time and use.

colorists Employees who work out different color combinations for fabric surface designs.

color scheme Plan for harmonious combination of colors.

commentary A spoken explanation of what is going on in a fashion show, especially pointing out specific features of each outfit being modeled.

commentator Fashion show narrator who interprets trends for the audience.

commercial pattern company A firm that designs, produces, packages, and sells patterns for home sewers.

Commercial Standards "Recorded voluntary standards of the trade." The U.S. Bureau of Standards issues Commercial Standards that are not laws, but are important as accepted voluntary benchmarks of performance and quality by the industry. These standards are usually referred to by number, and spell out test procedures and minimum performance deadlines.

commission Payment based on a percentage of the dollar amount of sales made by a hired person.

commissionaires Independent foreign buying agents who help retailers buy goods from their countries.

Committee for the Implementation of Textile Agreements (CITA) Government group that negotiates and administers individual agreements and quota programs.

commodity fibers Generic fibers not identified with any specific manufacturer.

commodity products   Staple goods that hardly ever change in design and are in constant demand.

comparable-store sales   An analysis of a retailer's sales in relation to close competitors that have similar store sizes, expense structures, merchandise lines, departmental structures, and ways of operating.

comparison shoppers   Retail employees who check the merchandise assortments, prices, ambiance, and services offered in competing and non-competing stores, as well as the advertising, displays, and knowledge and demeanor of salespeople.

complementary color scheme   Plan using hues across from each other on the color wheel.

completion date   The date designated by the retailer on the purchase order specifying when the goods are needed and should be delivered.

composite fabric   An engineered fabric made from two or more components. One component is often a strong fiber such as fiberglass or Kevlar, which gives the material its tensile strength, while another component (often called a matrix) is often a resin, such as polyester or epoxy that binds the fibers together.

computer-aided design (CAD)   An integrated computer system that aids in designing and pattern-making, used in both textile and apparel design.

computer-aided manufacturing (CAM)   Computerized pattern-making, grading, marker making, cutting, and sewing machines; essentially electronically controlled production.

computer-integrated manufacturing (CIM)   Computer connection to integrate computer-aided design and manufacturing systems.

computerized knife cutter   Electronically controlled machine that cuts multiple layers of fabrics into garment parts.

confined   Selling only to one retailer within a certain geographic trading area on an exclusive basis, or only to a particular chain of retail stores nationally.

consignment   Placing merchandise for sale in a store and being paid a percentage of the retail price if and when the merchandise is sold; the supplier retains ownership of the goods rather than the retailer taking title.

consolidated shopping   Merchandise for two or more companies are put together into a truckload to lower transportation costs.

consulting   The selling of a person's expert ideas and advice as a service business.

consumer   Someone who buys merchandise.

consumer credit   The use of credit cards or other purchase charges that allow consumers to merchandise immediately and pay for it later.

consumer demand   The effect consumers have on the marketplace.

consumer-direct retailing   Nonstore selling to consumers who shop from home.

consumer fashion shows   Fashion shows presented by retailers to consumers.

consumer obsolescence   The rejection of merchandise in favor of something new, even those the "old" still has utility.

consumer promotion   Promotion directly to consumers, usually done on a national scale by companies that do not sell directly to consumers.

continuous filament   A long, continuous, unbroken strand of fiber extruded from a spinneret in the form of a monofilament. Most manufactured fibers such as nylon, polyester, rayon, and acetate are made in a continuous filament form.

contractor   An independent producer who does the sewing (and sometimes the cutting) for manufacturers; an outside shop.

convenience goods   Necessities that consumers purchase regularly, with a minimum of shopping, from the most accessible retail outlets.

converter   A person or company that buys gray goods and sells them as finished fabrics. A converter organizes and manages the process of finishing the fabric to a buyer's specifications, particularly the bleaching, dyeing, printing, etc.

cooperative fashion shows   Jointly sponsored fashion shows, with expenses shared by two or more organization.

copywriter   A fashion writer who composes the word messages describing items promoted in advertisements, catalogs, and brochures.

corporate buying office   A resident buying office owned and financed by a store ownership group or syndicate.

corporation   A chartered enterprise organized as a separate legal entity with most of the legal rights of a person.

cosmetics   Products to be applied to the face, skin, or hair to improve appearance.

cost of goods sold (COGS)   An accounting of what has been spent on goods that have been sold to customers during the period.

costume curator   Person who locates, identifies, and determines the age of textiles, apparel, and accessories from the past.

costume jewelry   "Fashion jewelry" that is inexpensive, often made out of plated metals and artificial stones.

costume technician   Theatrical wardrobe helper who organizes the costumes and accessories by character and scene.

cottage industry   Manufacturing that uses labor of family units working in their homes with their own equipment.

cotton   A natural cellulosic fiber obtained from the boll of the cotton plant.

counterfeit fashions   Fashion goods with false producer labels or designer logos, also called knockoffs.

couture (koo-TOUR)   French word for dressmaking; applied to fashion businesses that make clothes to order. Custom-made designer segment of the fashion industry for the highest price "class" market.

couturier   High fashion designer.

Crafted With Pride in U.S.A. Council (CWP)   An industry-wide organization to strengthen the competitive position of the U.S. soft goods chain by conducting an ongoing "Buy American" campaign.

created audience   A fashion show audience that is established as a result of publicity and advertising after the show is planned.

croquis (kroh-KEE)   A rough preliminary drawing or a sketch.

cross-dyeing   Method of dyeing blend or combination fabrics to two or more shades by using dyes with different affinities for the various fibers.

cross-shopping   The consumer trend of combining purchases from both ends of the price scale.

culmination stage   The top popularity of the fashion cycle when a fashion is in great demand by almost everyone.

custom-made   Apparel made to a customer's special order; cut and fitted to individual measurements; the opposite of ready-to-wear.

Customs Service   U.S. agency responsible for keeping track of and enforcing trade barriers for points of entry into the country.

cutter   The person who cuts material during the manufacturing process.

cutter's must An itemized list of pattern piece components.

cyber-retailing The showing of a consumer's own images on the screen to see how specific clothing would look on him or her.

database marketing Using information about customer gathered from credit cards and other sources to plan marketing strategies.

decided customers Customers who know exactly what they want and why, preferring to make their purchase quickly.

décor The style and appearance of interior furnishings.

demand The amounts of a good or service that consumers are willing and able to buy at a certain time and price.

denier (den-YAY) Term to describe fiber (usually filament) thickness or diameter. Higher numbers indicate thicker threads.

departmental buyer A traditional department store employee who plans and purchases goods for only one department and is responsible for the sales and profits of the department.

department store General merchandise store, including apparel, household goods, and furniture, that offer many varieties of merchandise grouped into separate departments.

design A particular or unique vision of a style because of an original or individual arrangement of parts, form, color, line, and texture. Also, the plan used to put an idea together.

designer A person employed to create ideas for garments or accessories in the fashion industry.

designer patterns Patterns for replicas of actual designer fashions (such as Very Easy Very Vogue) offered to home sewers by commercial pattern companies.

designing The process if creating new versions of garments, accessories, and other items.

design stylist A person who redesigns existing garments rather than creating new fashion designs. Also, one who advises about styles in apparel and other categories of goods.

diffusion line An accessible ready-to-wear line for the masses produced by a major designer who usually sells expensive couture. Started when designers began creating diffusion lines (sometimes called secondary lines) of their own labels, like D&G by Dolce & Gabbana and Gianni Versace's Versace Jeans Couture. A more recent trend is for designers to create lines for discount chains and department store, like Mizrahi for Target and Vera Wang's Simply Vera line for Kohl's.

direct selling The exchange of merchandise to individual consumers in return for money or credit.

discount retailing Low-margin retailing; retailers able to offer inexpensive merchandise by buying in quantity and keeping operating costs low.

display Visual presentation of merchandise or ideas.

divisional merchandise manager (DMM) Retail executive who supervises a group of buyers and/or coordinated the merchandise of several related departments, divisions, or stores.

dobby attachment Loom attachment the permits the weaving of geometric figures.

domestic market centers Buying areas in one's own country.

domestics Bedding textiles (sheets, bedspreads, and blankets).

doors Fashion industry jargon for the number of retail stores at which a particular product is sold.

downsize The use of smaller size numbers for equal body measurements in expensive fashions. *See* vanity sizing.

downsizing The reduction of the size of a business to reduce costs and become more efficient.

double knit A weft knit fabric in which two layers of loops are formed that cannot be separated. A double knit machine, which has two complete sets of needles, is required for this construction.

draping A method of making a pattern by draping fabric on a dress form.

dress code A set of written or unwritten rules of appropriate attire.

dressers People who help fashion show models change and care for the clothes.

dressmakers/tailors Expert sewers who make custom garments or do apparel alterations and repairs.

dressmaker's dummy A model or replica of the human form, used for displaying or fitting clothes.

durable finish Fabric finish that lasts through several launderings or dry cleanings but loses its effectiveness over a period of time.

dyeing Method of giving color to a fiber, yard, fabric, or garment with either natural or synthetic dyes.

edit When a manufacturer changes or revises the designs in an apparel line, or a retail buyer prioritizes the available goods for a buying plan.

electronic article surveillance (EAS) A shoplifting prevention system that uses specially designed tags containing a small circuit that emits a signal that, if not deactivated, is sensed by devices at exits.

electronic retailing Shop-by-computer retailing.

electronic storefront A computer-simulated store that consumers can scroll through by aisle, product, category, or item.

embroidery An embellishment of a fabric or garment in which colored threads are sewn on to the fabric to create a design. May be done either by hand or by machine.

ergonomics The study of improving a garment design by enhancing the wearer's comfort, performance, or health.

emphasis Principle of design that uses a concentration of interest in a particular part or area of a design.

environmental consultant Environmental consultants work on commercial contracts to address a variety of environmental issues for their clients. They may assess air, land, and water contamination, waste management, help develop environmental policies and management systems.

e-tailing An industry buzz word signifying electronic retailing.

ethics Acting or dealing in good morally evaluated ways.

evening wear Evening attire and accessories for women, including ball gowns and other types of formal garments.

everyday low pricing (EDLP) Retail strategy of consistently offering fair prices and good values at all times.

executive trainee programs General orientation offered by most large companies for new employees with college degrees. Also called management training programs.

export merchants Foreign wholesalers who specialize in efficiently exporting goods from their countries.

export trading companies (ETCs) Intermediaries between U.S. exporters and foreign buyers.

extenders "Multipliers" that can be mixed and matched within a wardrobe for more outfits.

fabricated products Sewn garments, accessories, and other manufactured items.

fabrication Selection of the appropriate fabric for a garment.

fabrications Fabrics, leathers, furs, or other materials used in making fashion products.

fabric librarian Employee of a manufactured fiber company, natural fiber trade association, or home sewing pattern company who is in charge of the fabric library.

fabric library   A collection of sample fabrics for the upcoming fashion season

fabrics   Long pieces of cloth.

fabric structural designers   Textile company employees who interpret fashion into new woven or knitted patterns.

factory outlet stores   Stores that sell manufacturers' overruns directly to the consumer.

fad   A temporary, passing fashion that has a great appeal to many people for a short period of time.

fashion   The styles presented each season that are adopted and worn by the majority of a demographic group.

Fashion Avenue   The part of Seventh Avenue that runs through the Garment District in Manhattan, officially named in 1972 in honor of the famed fashion designers who helped establish New York City as a fashion capital.

fashion consultant   *See* personal shopper.

fashion cycle   The ongoing rise, peak, and fall in popularity of specific styles or shapes.

fashion designers   Employees who create ideas that combine function and beauty into new garments.

fashion director   The fashion expert of an organization, who keeps it current with fashion developments and works with designers or buyers to form the fashion image of a company.

fashion editor   The head fashion reporter at a magazine or newspaper who analyzes the fashion scene and interprets it for readers.

fashion educator   Person who gives instruction on school clothing and merchandising classes, extension work, and adult and consumer education courses.

fashion followers   Individuals who wear a fashion look only when it is firmly accepted.

On the Cutting Edge

Tech Savvy

New technology related to the fashion business is developing every day. By the time this book is published, many more high-tech terms will have become current, and some listed here may already be outdated. Be sure you keep abreast of the latest technologies in fashion by reading the technology sections in industry trade journals. Blogs often contain the latest news, but are not always reliable sources of information.

fashion forecast   A prediction of fashion trends.

fashion look   A total accessorized outfit.

fashion magazines   Magazines for consumers that have international fashion emphasis through articles, illustrations, and advertisements.

fashion marketing   The making and selling of apparel and accessories that are desirable to consumers.

fashion merchandising   The planning required to have the right fashion merchandise available in the proper quantities and place at the right time and priced to meet consumer demand.

fashion models   People who wear garments and accessories to promote them.

fashion movement   Ongoing change in what is considered to be fashionable.

fashion piracy   The stealing of design ideas.

fashion press   Reporters of fashion news for magazines such as *Vogue* and *Marie Claire*, trade papers such as *Women's Wear Daily*, and for newspapers, such as the Styles section of the *New York Times*.

fashion products   Goods that are always changing, having style and timing risk.

fashion retailing   The business of buying fashion merchandise from a variety of sources and reselling it to ultimate consumers at a convenient location or via the Internet, television, or catalogs.

fashion seasons   Retail selling periods.

fashion shows   Theatrical presentations of apparel, accessories, and other fashion products on live models to audiences.

fashion trend   New direction in fashion styling.

fashion weeks   *See* Market weeks.

fast fashion   A term used to describe clothing collections based on the most recent fashion trends presented at Fashion Week in both the spring and fall. These trends are manufactured quickly, and in a affordable way, to allow consumers to take advantage of current clothing styles at a lower price. Stores such as H&M, Forever 21, and Zara are considered fast fashion retailers.

Fédération Française de la Couture   French couture trade association composed of three main membership classifications (each called a Chambre Syndicale) and associated groups of manufacturers and artisans.

fiber   The basic entity, either natural or manufactured, which is twisted into yarns and then used in the production of a fabric.

findings   Any extra items attached to the garment during the manufacturing process. This can include trims, buttons, hooks, snaps, or embellishments.

finished goods   Completed, post-production manufactured items.

finishers   Apparel production employees who do hand work to finish better quality, higher-priced garments.

finishing   The last treatments given to fabrics; the final handiwork or final touches done to a garment.

first cost   The wholesale price for goods in a foreign country of origin, exclusive of shipping costs and duties.

first pattern   Trial pattern made in the design department for a sample garment.

fit model   A design room or showroom model who tries on and models samples for the company's management and retail buyers.

fittings   Before a fashion show, the trying on of merchandise by models to see how each garment looks and fits.

fitting sheet   A written form for each lineup number in a fashion show.

flagship store   Largest and most representative store in a chain organization.

flats   Flattened sketches of a garment accompanied by all specifics such as size, fabrication, details such as trim, closures. Once made by hand, but now most flats are produced digitally.

floor-ready merchandise (FRM)   Vendor-shipped items in a condition to be put directly on the retail shelf or fixture without any additional preparation.

focus group   A dozen or so people in a room with a facilitator who leads a discussion about a particular subject of product line while company representatives watch to gain feedback.

footwear   Accessories that include dress shoes, casual shoes, boots, slippers, and athletic shoes.

ford   A style of design that is produced at the same time by many different manufacturers at many different prices.

forecasting services   Consultants that foresee the colors, textures, and silhouettes, to predict coming fashion trends.

franchising   When a manufacturer sells the rights to retail its merchandise.

free trade A government's policy of allowing goods to flow freely in and out of its economy without interference.

full-fashioned knits Knit garments with pieces shaped on the knitting machine.

full-service retailing Stores with salespeople who assist customers one-to-one in every phase of the shopping process.

furnishings Men's clothing category, including shirts, accessories, and item sportswear.

furrier Manufacturer of fur items.

garment An article of wearing apparel such as a dress, suit, coat, evening gown, or sweater.

garment district Area within a fashion city where most of the apparel companies are located.

garment dyeing The dyeing of constructed garments by apparel manufacturers to fill retail orders for requested colors.

GATT (General Agreement on Tariffs and Trade) A former contract between governments to provide a secure international trading environment, now replaced by the World Trade Organization (WTO).

gauge A measurement most commonly associated with knitting equipment. It can mean the number of needles per inch in a knitting machine. However, in full-fashioned hosiery and sweater machines, the number of needles per 1-1/2 inches represents the gauge.

general merchandise manager (GMM) High-level retail executive responsible for the total retail merchandising operation.

girls' sizes Apparel sizes from 7–16, for girls of those corresponding ages.

globalization The trend for manufacturers and retailers (and all businesses) to expand throughout the world.

go-see A scheduled meeting when a model is scrutinized to determine if she or he fits the look that the company wants.

grading Process of making a sample size pattern larger and smaller to make up a complete size range.

grain The direction of the lengthwise and crosswise yarns or threads in a woven fabric.

greige goods An unfinished fabric, just removed from a knitting machine or a loom. Also called grey goods.

half-sizes Apparel sizes for heavier, short-waisted women.

hand   The way a fabric feels when it is touched. Terms like softness, crispness, dryness, and silkiness are all terms that describe the hand of the fabric.

hang tag   Detachable heavy paper signs that are affixed to the outside of garments as a form of promotion to help sell products.

haute couture   A French term applied to the original garments or high fashions, designed by couture houses. Haute couture fashions are distinguished by luxury fabrics, fine detailing, hand sewing, and custom fit.

header   Large swatches of fabric (approximately 12 inches square) that show pattern, fabric content, name of textile mill, weight, as well as other available color combinations.

headwear   Hats and caps, sometimes called millinery.

heather   A yarn that is spun using pre-dyed fibers. These fibers are blended together to give a particular look. (For instance black and white may be blended to create a gray heathered yarn.) The term is also used to describe fabric made from heathered yarn.

hemp   A coarse, durable bast fiber obtained from the inner bark of the hemp plant.

herringbone   A variation on the twill weave construction in which the twill is reversed, or broken, at regular intervals, producing a zigzag effect.

high fashion   Items of the very latest or newest fashions; high style.

home sewing industry   Businesses that deal with the production and selling of non-industrial sewing machines, notions, and retail fabrics, patterns, and publications.

hosiery   Stockings, including pantyhose, tights, knee highs, leg warmers, and all other socks.

houndstooth check   A variation on the twill weave construction in which a broken check effect is produced by a variation in the pattern of interlacing yarns, utilizing at least two different colored yarns.

house boutique   Small retail shop owned by a couturier that sells items with the couturier's label.

Ideacomo   Italian fabric producers' trade fair, held each November and May in Como, Italy, followed by presentations in New York.

ideal chart   A fashion show planning device that names all merchandise categories to be presented and the number of garments to be selected per category.

importers Merchants that bring in products from overseas.

imports Goods made in a foreign country.

infants' apparel Clothing for babies and toddlers younger than three years old.

initial markup The difference between merchandise cost and the selling price originally placed on the merchandise.

inside shop Apparel firm that does all stages of garment production itself, from design concept and fabric purchasing, through all sewing procedures, to the shipment of finished garments.

inspectors/trimmers Apparel manufacturing employees who cut off loose threads, pull out basting stitches, and remove lint and spots from garments.

intensity The dullness or brightness of a color.

Internet sales Retail transactions made through the Internet with home computers.

internships Work-study programs at the college level.

intimate apparel The general women's category that includes foundation garments, lingerie, and loungewear.

inventory Goods held on hand for the production process or to be sold to customers.

inventory control The process of maintaining inventories at a level that prevents stockout and minimizes holding costs.

inventory management Activities that ensure a flow of merchandise from vendors to stores to consumers; stock control.

irregulars Items with imperfections, such as slight mistakes in manufacturing.

Jacquard Woven fabrics manufactured by using the Jacquard attachment on the loom. Brocade and damask are types of jacquard woven fabrics.

Jacquard loom Machine that weaves large and intricate designs with a series of programmed punch cards.

jersey, jersey fabric The consistent interlooping of yarns in the jersey stitch produces a fabric with a smooth, flat face and a more textured but uniform back.

jobber A middleman between the producer and the commercial consumer.

junior Size range of female apparel for fully developed, small-boned and short-waisted females; in odd numbers 3–15.

knit fabric Fabrics made from only one set of yarns, all running in the same direction. Some knits have their yarns running along the length of the fabric, while others have their yarns running across the width of the fabric. Knit fabrics are held together by looping the yarns around each other. Knitting creates ridges in the resulting fabric. Wales are the ridges that run lengthwise in the fabric; courses run crosswise.

knock-off A copy of another, usually higher-priced style or garment.

label Small pieces of ribbon or cloth attached to garments on the inside that contain printed information.

labor intensive Requiring many workers to make the products, rather than relying heavily on machines and technology.

lamb's wool The first clip of wool sheared from lambs up to eight months old. The wool is soft, slippery, and resilient. It is used in fine-grade woolen fabrics.

layaway A deferred purchase arrangement in which the store sets aside a customer's merchandise until the customer has fully paid for it.

leased department Area within a retail store that is stocked and operated by someone else.

licensed merchandise stores Concept shops built around licensed merchandise.

licensing Arrangement whereby a manufacturer is given the exclusive right to produce and market goods that bear the famous name of someone who, in return, receives a percentage of wholesale sales. The person may or may not take an active role in the design of the products being produced.

line An apparel manufacturer's collection of styles and designs that will be produced and sold as a set of new selections for a given season; also visual direction in a design caused by seams, details, or trimming.

line buying Buying lines from reputable manufacturers.

linen A fabric made from linen fibers obtained from inside the woody stem of the flax plant. Linen fibers are much stronger and more lustrous than cotton. Linen fabrics are very cool and absorbent but the wrinkle easily unless blended with manufactured fibers. Linen is one of the oldest textile fibers.

lineup The order in which outfits will appear in a fashion show.

long-run fashions Styles that take a long time to complete the fashion cycle.

look book Straightforward images of fully styled looks from a designer's latest collection. Shot against a simple and uncomplicated background. Usually 5 x 7, bound.

loom   A machine used for weaving fabrics.

loss leader   An item sold at less than the regular wholesale price for the purpose of attracting retail buyers to other merchandise.

Lyocell   New type of solvent-spun cellulosic fiber. Lyocell has a similar hand and drape as rayon but it is stronger, more durable, and in many cases machine washable. It has a subtle luster and is rich in color. It also resists shrinkage, and absorbs well, and is wrinkle resistant.

madras   A lightweight plain weave cotton fabric with a striped, plaid, or checked pattern. A true madras will bleed when washed. This type of fabric is usually imported from India. End uses are men's and women's shirts and dresses.

magalogue   A catalog designed to look like a magazine, used as a marketing tool.

MAGIC   Men's Apparel Guild in California, the world's largest men's apparel trade show, held each February and August in Las Vegas.

mail-order retailers   Companies that sell through catalogs they distribute to consumers. Also called direct-mail marketers.

mannequins   Lifelike human forms, used to display apparel in retail stores.

mannequin work   Employment as a model for a designer or manufacturer to check fit and show samples.

manufactured fibers   Fibers created through technology and produced artificially from substances such as cellulose, petroleum, and chemicals.

maquiladoras   Mexican plants just across the U.S. border used for less expensive production.

markdown   The difference between the original retail price and a reduced price.

marker   A pattern layout put on top of the fabric for the cutter to follow.

markers   Apparel manufacturing employees who figure out how the pattern pieces can be placed most efficiently for cutting.

market   A group of potential customers, or the place, area, or time at which buys and sellers meets to transact business.

market coverage   The amount of concentration a retailer has in a customer area, such as intensive, selective, or exclusive.

market driven   Responding to market or consumer needs.

marketing   The process of planning, promoting, and selling merchandise.

marketing chain   The flow of product development, production, and distribution from concept to consumer.

marketing manager   Executive who plans and directs all marketing endeavors of a company.

market research   The process of systematically gathering and analyzing information, such as consumer tastes and changing trends, relating to particular market.

market weeks   Scheduled periods of time during which producers officially introduce their new lines of merchandise and retail buyers shop the various lines.

markup   Difference between cost price and selling price.

mass fashion   Styles that are produced in volume and widely sold at lower prices.

mass merchandiser   Retailer who sells mass-produced fashions at moderate to low price points.

mass production   The production of merchandise in quantity.

materials handling   All activities of goods not involved in actual production processes, such as moving, storing, packing, and transporting of the raw materials, semi-finished parts, or final garments.

matrix brands   Key suppliers of department stores.

mercerization   A process of treating a cotton yarn or fabric, in which the yarn or fabric is immersed in a caustic soda solution and later neutralized in acid. The process causes a permanent swelling of the fiber, resulting in an increased luster on the surface of the fabric, and increased affinity for dyes, and an increased strength.

merchandise blend   The right products being at the right place at the right time in the right quantity at the right price with the right appeal.

merchandise manager   Employee who coordinates the merchandise of several retail departments.

merchandise planning   Activities of estimating consumer demand and how it can best be satisfied.

merchandiser   An individual responsible for researching the fashion preferences of a company's target customer and directing the creative process of the designer to ensure the designs developed are consistent with the customer's preferences.

merchandising   The process through which products are obtained (designed, developed, or bought for resale) and promoted to the point of sale, trying to match those products to established market requirements to make a profit.

merchandising cycle   A circle of ongoing planning, buying, and selling activity.

merchandising director   Executive who figures out what the company's customers will want.

merino   A type of wool that originates from purebred Merino sheep. The best Merino wool comes from Italy.

microfibers   The name given to ultra-fine manufactured fibers and the name given to the technology of developing these fibers. Fibers made using micro fiber technology produce fibers that weigh less that 1.0 denier. The fabrics made from these extra-fine fibers have a superior hand, a gentle drape, and incredible softness. Microfibers are two times finer than silk, three times finer than cotton, and one hundred times finer than a human hair.

misses   Apparel size category for fully developed women of average height, weight, and proportions.

moda pronta   Italian ready-to-wear.

mode or moda   Synonym for fashion; used mainly in Europe.

model   *See* fashion model.

model lineup sheets   Individual forms for each model in a fashion show, giving the order of appearance, outfits, and other details.

mohair   Hair fibers from the Angora goat. Items made from mohair include sweaters, coats, suits, and scarves.

mood board   A presentation board that shows the overall concept and direction of a design collection. It captures the style and theme for a set of designs by displaying defining images, fabrics, and colors that are influential in the design process.

Multifiber Arrangement (MFA)   A bilateral agreement among exporting and importing nations that provides the framework to prevent import surges.

multinational corporations (MNCs)   Companies that operate globally with direct investment in several different companies.

muslin (1)   An inexpensive, medium weight, plain weave, low thread count cotton sheeting fabric. Commonly used in fashion design to make trial garments for preliminary fit.

muslin (2)   A test garment produced out of inexpensive muslin fabric.

nap   A fuzzy, furlike feel created when fiber ends extend from the basic fabric structure to the fabric surface. The fabric can be napped on either or both sides.

national brands Manufacturers' brands that are available nationwide.

natural fibers Textile strands from plants and animals.

needle trades Term referring to the garment manufacturing, or apparel, industry.

neutrals Black, white, and gray rather than true hues.

never-outs Best-selling merchandise items that account for a significant sales volume and must always be available.

niche marketing The production of specific lines of goods for carefully defined customers.

North American Free Trade Agreement (NAFTA) Trade agreement, implemented in 1994, creating a free market between the United States, Mexico, and Canada.

nylon Produced in 1938, the first completely synthetic fiber developed. Known for its high strength and excellent resilience, nylon has superior abrasion resistance and high flexibility.

offshore assembly Fabric purchased and cut in the United States, but sent to Mexico or the Caribbean countries for sewing.

offshore production Manufacturing that is done overseas.

one-off A one-of-a-kind piece.

outside shop Apparel firm that handles everything but the sewing and sometimes the cutting, using contractors to do those productions steps.

outsourcing The hiring of independent specialists to do particular work, rather than using company employees.

overhead The costs of operating the store or company.

overlock machine A machine with needle and loopers that creates an edge finish while sewing a seam.

oxford A fine, soft, lightweight woven cotton or blended with manufactured fibers used primarily in shirtings.

paisley A tear-drop-shaped, fancy printed pattern used in dresses, blouses, and men's ties.

pattern graders Manufacturing employees who cut patterns in all the different sizes produced by the manufacturer.

pattern makers Manufacturing employees who cut patterns in all the different sizes produced by the manufacturer.

peau de soie A heavy, twill weave drapeable satin fabric, made of silk or a manufactured fiber, and used for bridal gowns and evening wear.

performance fabrics   High-tech fabrics, using interesting fiber blends and finishes, to create durable and flexible fabrics that provide functional qualities such as moisture management, UV protection, anti-microbial, thermo-regulation, and wind and water resistance.

permanent press   Term used to describe a garment that has been treated to retain its fresh appearance, crease, and shape throughout the life of the garment. Permanent press can be a misleading description, because no finish is completely permanent. "Durable press" or "crease resistant" are the more accepted terms.

petite   Apparel size category for short females.

physical inventory   A physical count of stock at hand.

piece goods   The trade term for fabrics.

piecework   Manufacturing in which one specific task is assigned to each person along an assembly line; also rate by which many factory workers are paid.

plaid   A pattern consisting of colored bars of stripes that cross each other at right angles, comparable with a Scottish tartan.

plant capacity   The quantity of garments that can be made in a factory at a certain time.

pleat   A portion of fabric folded over and secured by stitching or pressing.

ply   Two or more yarns that have been twisted together.

point-of-sale (POS)   Merchandise data collected electronically when consumer purchase transactions are recorded.

polyester   A manufactured fiber introduced in the 1950s, second only to cotton in worldwide use. Polyester has high strength, excellent resiliency, and high abrasion resistance. Low absorbancy allows the fiber to dry quickly.

pop-up retail   A temporary retail manifestation; a store that opens quickly, often unannounced, quickly draws crowds, and then disappears or morphs into something else. Examples of this trend include the temporary floating store on the Hudson River that Target opened up for the 2003 Christmas season, and the real-world outlet store that the online retailer Bluefly.com opened in New York.

portfolio   A case of loose, unfolded art or design papers showing a person's creative work.

Première-Vision   French term for "first look;" international fabric trade fair held each March and October in Paris.

pressers Apparel industry employees who flatten seams, iron garment surfaces, and shape garments with team-pressing machines.

press show Private fashion showing for the press before the public sees the fashions.

prêt à porter French term for ready-to-wear collections produced in France. French prêt à porter retains aspects of haute couture while integrating manufacturing techniques of mass merchandisers.

preticketing Ticketing of merchandise by the manufacturer so that the merchandise is ready for prompt distribution at the retail store.

price line A specific price point at which an assortment of merchandise is offered for sale.

price point The dollar amount at which an item is offered for sale.

price range The range between the lowest and the highest price lines carried.

printing Process for adding color, pattern, or design to the surface of fabrics.

private labeling Private label clothing is clothing that is manufactured by one company and sold under the brand of another. Every major retailer owns at least a few of their own private label brands.

product data management systems (PDM) Computer software systems used to organize and edit a line.

product development A team approach utilized by manufacturers to design product lines targeted to specific customers. The design term typically comprises a merchandiser, a designer, and a project manager.

production pattern The final pattern made to company size standards.

production show The most elaborate and expensive type of fashion show, with entertainment, backdrops, and lighting effects.

promotion Products offered at special prices.

prophetic fashions Styles that are identified early as future best sellers in many price ranges.

proportion The relation of one part of a design to another; an important principle of garment design.

purchase order (PO) A written document authorizing the delivery of certain goods at specific prices and times.

Quick Response (QR) An industry-wide program that ties together the entire textile/apparel pipeline using barcode data, EDI technology, and long-term customer-supplier partnerships.

Radio Frequency Identification (RFID) A small electronic device that consists of a small chip with an antenna, included on, among other things, anti-theft tags attached to merchandise in stores. RIFD technology has the potential to make the supply chain of goods far more efficient, since RIFD readers on shelves could monitor how many goods are being sold and signal to inventory when more stock is needed.

rag trade Old insiders' term for the garment manufacturing industry.

ramie A natural vegetable fiber from the stem of a nettle-like shrub.

rayon A man-made fiber made from rejuvenated cellulose, derived from wood pulp, cotton linters, or other vegetable matter.

ready-to-wear Apparel manufactured in factories based on standardized measurements and size classifications; mass-produced rather than custom made.

receiving The area of the store where packages are opened, checked, and marked.

refabricate Apparel designs with high sales volumes in the previous season, which are retained for the next season with only minor changes.

regional manager Chain retailer executive who oversees several districts.

repeat The repetition of a print in a fabric design.

resource Term used by retailers for a manufacturer, wholesaler, vendor, or distributor; or a source for ideas or information.

retailer A business that sells goods purchased from wholesalers and manufacturers to the ultimate consumer.

retailing The business of buying goods at wholesale markets or producing goods and selling them to the ultimate consumer.

retail price The wholesale price plus a markup covering the retailer's operating costs and a profit.

rub-off A garment whose measurements are used as the basis for creating a new garment; a shortcut in design.

runner A best-selling style that sells in large quantities at all price levels.

runway Elevated fashion-show walkway for models that projects out from the stage, usually into the audience seating area.

runway model   A model who works in front of live audiences.

sales per square foot   Amount sold per square foot of store floor space; a measure of productivity.

sales presentations   Formal, well-prepared showings of a company's goods to potential customers.

sales quotas   Projected volumes of sales (units or dollars) assigned to a selling department or person for a certain time period.

sample   A trial garment or prototype made up exactly as they will look when sold.

sample cut   A three- to 10-yard length of fabric used by the design department to make up a trial sample garment.

sartorial   From the Latin *sartor*, which means tailor. Of or relating to a tailor or tailored clothes.

Savile Row   A street in London famous for its men's tailors.

seamless knitting   A process of circular knitting that essentially produces finished garments with no side seams, which require only minimal sewing to complete the garment.

seasonal products   Products that change in popularity or demand with the seasons of the year.

secondary lines   Ready-to-wear collections of renowned designers.

seconds   Merchandise factory rejects with defects that may affect wearability.

seersucker   A woven fabric that incorporates modification of tension control. In the production of seersucker, some of the warp threads are held under controlled tension at all times during the weaving, while other warp threads are in a relaxed state and tend to pucker when the filling yarns are placed. The result is a puckered stripe effect in the fabric. Seersucker is traditionally made into summer sportswear such as shirts, trousers, and informal suits.

selected distribution   Limiting the number of stores that may buy merchandise to maintain exclusivity.

self-help features   Attributes of garments that enable children, as well as people with disabilities and older people, to dress themselves.

selling areas   Store layout areas where merchandise is displayed and customers interact with sales personnel.

sell-through   The ability of a line to sell regularly and steadily at full price.

selvage   The thin compressed edge of woven fabric that runs parallel to the warp yarns and prevents raveling.

serge   A fabric with a smooth hand that is created by a two-up, two-down twill weave.

serging   An overcasting technique done on the cut edge of a fabric to prevent raveling.

Seventh Avenue   The main street of New York's Garment District; the term is used to represent the whole district; also called Fashion Avenue.

short-run fashions   Styles that are popular for a brief period of time, usually for only one selling season.

shoulder-out   A way of selling garments with only one side showing from shoulder to bottom.

showroom   A place where sales representatives or management show a line of merchandise to potential buyers; called *salons de presentations* in France.

silhouette   Outline of a garment.

silk   The only natural fiber in filament form; obtained from cocoons spun by silkworms. All silk comes from Asia, primarily China.

sketchers   Apparel company employees who do freehand drawings of ideas that designers have draped on to mannequins in fabric.

smart textiles   Textiles that can sense and react to changes in the environment, such as changes from mechanical, thermal, chemical, magnetic, and other sources.

soft goods   Fashion and textile merchandise.

soft goods chain   The channel of distribution for apparel and home decorating textiles.

sourcing   Worldwide search for the best available fabrics or garment production at the best price.

sourcing consultants   Experts hired to guide companies to identify countries and factories that give the best opportunities for their apparel production.

spandex   A man-made fiber of long-chain synthetic polymer comprised of stretchable segmented polyurethane; known best by the DuPont brand name of Lycra; it can be repeatedly stretched over 500 percent without breaking, and will still recover its original length.

special events   Activities set up to attract customers to a selling place.

specialty goods   Merchandise items that are well known to consumers by brand identification, high quality, or other specific characteristics.

specialty store   A retail establishment that handles narrow categories of goods, such as men's apparel, female apparel, or shoes.

spinning   The process of extruding and hardening man-made fibers; the process of drawing and twists staple fibers together into yarn or thread.

sportswear   Clothing designed for comfort or casual wear.

standard allowed hours   The time it takes to complete each assembly operation or garment.

stock keeping unit (SKU)   Number of styles that company will manufacture as well as the number of different colors each style will come in; the smallest unit for which sales and stock records are kept.

stock turnover   The number of times a store's merchandise stock is sold and replaced in a given period.

stone-washing   A textile manufacturing process that gives newly manufactured cloth a worn-out appearance. Also helps create softness and flexibility of otherwise stiff fabrics such as denim and canvas. The process uses large stone stones to roughen up the fabric being processed. Stone-washed jeans are created by washing jeans with pumice in a rotating drum, or by using chemicals to create the same effect. These were a popular fashion trend in the 1980s.

store image   The character or personality that the store presents to the public.

store wrap   Putting customer purchases in a distinctive store box, bag, or wrapping paper of particular color and design.

story   Design theme comprising fabric, color, or style associations that are used within particular collection.

style   Certain characteristics that distinguish a garment from other garments; a particular look in fashion.

style number   Number assigned to a particular apparel design that identifies it for manufacturing, retail ordering, and distribution.

style ranges   Categories of style that appeal to different consumers.

stylist   A fashion expert; generally selects colors, prints, or styles for presentation or prepares fashion merchandise for photographic presentation in an advertisement or catalog.

subcontractor   An individual or a business that signs a contract to perform part or all of the obligations of another's contract.

suit separates   Jackets and trousers or skirts that mix and match into many different outfits.

supply chain   The network of manufacturers, wholesalers, distributors, and retailers who turn raw materials into finished goods and services and deliver them to consumers.

sweeteners   New items added to a manufacturer's line between designing seasons.

tailor system   Manufacturing system in which all sewing tasks to make a garment are all done by a single operator.

tanning   The process of transforming animal skins into leather.

target market   The group of consumers to whom a producer, manufacturer, or retailer aims products, services, and advertising.

tea-room modeling   Presenting fashions informally by walking from table to table in a restaurant to show and tell about what is being worn. Very popular in the 1980s.

tear strength   The force necessary to tear a fabric, measured by the force necessary to start of continue a tear in fabric. Expressed in pounds or in grams. The most commonly used method to determine tear strength is the Elmendorf tear test procedure.

tech pack   A packet of technical specifications (also called a spec package) sent to a factory for each new style. Tech packs include the following forms and often others: a lead/sketch sheet, a specification measurement sheet, and a fabric and trim sheet.

television retailing   Selling to consumers by showing and describing merchandise on certain television channels.

tensile strength   The strength shown by a fiber, yarn, or fabric to resist breaking under pressure. It is the actual number of pounds of resistance that a fabric will give before the material is broken on the testing machine.

textile fabrics   Cloth made from textile fibers by weaving, knitting, felting, crocheting, lamination, or bonding.

textile performance   How a fabric performs, measured by durability, colorfastness, stain resistance, and other attributes.

thread count   The number of ends and picks per inch in a woven cloth; the number of wales and courses in a knit fabric.

toile (*twahl*)   The French word for a muslin sample garment.

trademark   Company's individual mark and name for a product.

trade shows   Periodic temporary exhibits schedules throughout the year in various trading centers.

trend book   A color publication that outlines the predicted future trends up to two years ahead.

trend buying   Retailers buy from new resources to obtain fashion newness.

trendsetter   A designer or fashion leader who sets a fashion direction that others follow.

trimmings   The decorative materials of fashion items, such as buttons, laces, belts, braids, etc. that are added to enhance the design.

trunk show   A show of designer clothes that moves from store to store, often accompanied by a personal appearance by the designer.

tweed   A medium-to-heavy-weight fluffy, woolen, twill weave fabric containing colored slubbed yarns. Commonly used to make coats and suits.

unit control   Systems for recording the number of units of merchandise bought, sold, in stock, or on order.

Best Practice

Terminology

Using correct terminology identifies you as an insider and shows you are familiar with the business. Fiona is a buyer for a sportswear line who wants to move into a higher-paying position as a divisional merchandise manager. One good way to show that she is ready for the additional responsibility of that position is to demonstrate, in the course of an interview or an informal discussion, that she is conversant with the vocabulary of that position. Also being able to speak knowledgeably about retail theory can help convince those in charge of hiring that Fiona is ready for the job.

unit production systems (UPS)   Computer-guided conveyers that move garments automatically from one work station to the next; automatic progressive-bundle system.

UNITE   Union of Needletrades, Industrial and Textile Employees.

universal product codes (UPC)   Standard codes that identify style, color, size, price, fabrication, and vendor on price tags and enable this information to be fed through an electronic data interchange system.

value pricing   The selling of items below the price suggested by vendors of the goods.

vanity sizing   Also known as size inflation occurs when clothing is sized smaller to please the customer, by taking all garments down a size.

vendor   A seller, resource, manufacturer, or supplier.

vertical integration   The joining of companies at different levels of production and marketing, such as a fiber producer with a fabric mill; the combining of two or more steps of the pipeline within one company and under one management.

virgin wool   New wool that has never been used before or reclaimed from any spun, woven, knitted, felted, manufactured or used products.

virtual showrooms   Showing a manufacturer's line on the Internet.

viscose   The most common type of rayon.

visual merchandising   Making merchandise visually attractive to customers.

warp   In woven fabric, the yarns that run lengthwise and are interwoven with the fill (weft) yarns.

wash-and-wear   Ability of a garment to be washed by hand or in a washing machine and require little or no ironing. Also referred to as "easy care."

weaving   The process of forming fabric by interlacing yarns on looms. The three basic weaves are plain, twill, and satin. All other weaves, no matter how intricate, use one or more of these basic weaves in their composition.

weft   In woven fabric, the filling yarns that run perpendicular to the warp yarns.

weight of cloth   Describes the variety of ways that fabric is sold: ounces per linear yard, yards per pound, or ounces per square yard.

wheel of retailing theory   An evolutionary process in which stores that feature low prices gradually upgrade themselves.

white goods   A very broad term that implies any goods bleached and finished in the white condition. Some of the cotton white goods are muslin, cambric, dimity, lawn, organdy, voile, etc.

wholesale market   A market where commercial consumers buy in large quantities from producers.

wholesale price   The price paid by commercial consumers for supplies and products.

wholesaler A distributor or vendor who purchases large quantities of goods from a manufacturer and sells small quantities to retailers.

wicking Dispersing or spreading of moisture or liquid through a given area by capillary action in the material.

window dresser Employee who does window displays. Also called window trimmer.

winners Best-selling items in a manufacturer's line that are recut for production the next season.

women's Apparel size category for females with larger proportions.

Women's Wear Daily Trade publication of the women's fashion industry.

wool Usually associated with a fiber or fabric made from the fleece of sheep or lamb. However, the term *wool* can also apply to animal hair fibers, including the hair of the Cashmere or Angora goat or the specialty hair fibers of the camel, alpaca, llama, or vicuna.

woolen Less expensive wool fabric, made of short fibers, that is relatively dense and has a soft, fuzzy surface.

World Trade Organization (WTO) The governing body of international trade, which replaced GATT.

yarns Continuous strands of textile fibers spun into a form suitable for processing into fabrics.

zori A flat thonged sandal usually made of straw, cloth, leather, or rubber.

Chapter 6

Resources

This chapter provides resources used by those in all levels and positions in the fashion industry. Associations and organizations are excellent places to begin networking, and many offer educational seminars. The books highlighted can help build your knowledge of the history of the fashion world, as well as provide general career advice. Periodicals are an excellent way of staying current with the business—knowledge that is very important to have when going into job interviews. Educational institutions of both the traditional "brick-and-mortar" and online models can help confer credentials necessary to advance your career. Utilize Web sites to forecast trends and access databases of source materials. Finally, "Other Media" features films—some serious exposés of the industry, others lighter in fare—that take on the world of fashion.

Associations and Organizations

A number of organizations and institutions offer invaluable information and resources to those in the trade. Take a look at some of these.

Professional

Staying current is essential in this industry. Anyone in fashion can find a few useful contacts in this list.

American Apparel and Footwear Association (AAFA) is a national trade association representing all types of U.S. apparel, footwear, and other sewn products companies. (http://www.apparelandfootwear.org)

American Association of Textile Chemists and Colorists (AATCC) is the world's leading not-for-profit association serving textile professionals. AATCC provides test method development, quality control materials, and professional networking for thousands of members in 60 countries. (http://www.aatcc.org)

American Fiber Manufacturers Association, Inc. (AFMA) is a trade organization founded in 1933 for producers of manufactured fibers in the United States. (http://www.fibersource.com/afma/afma.htm)

American Marketing Association (AMA) is the largest marketing association in North America. This is a professional organization for individuals and organizations involved in the practice, teaching, and studying of marketing worldwide. A source of information, resources, education and training and professional networking. (http://www.marketingpower.com)

American Textile Manufacturers Institute (ATMI) is a large and influential national trade organization for the U.S. textile industry. The ATMI is the industry's primary spokesperson with the legislative and administrative branches of the federal government as well as the news media. (http://www.textileweb.com)

British Fashion Council (BFC) promotes leading British fashion designers in the global market and develops London's position as a major player in the international fashion arena. Organizers of the annual British Fashion Awards. (http://www.britishfashioncouncil.com)

Clothing Manufacturers' Association of the U.S.A. (CMA) is an association for manufacturers of men's and boys' tailored clothing. Provides assistance to members on labor and government relations and sponsors seminars and conferences.

Computer Integrated Textile Design Association (CITDA) is an association committed to the use, management, and development of computer-integrated design (CIA) and computer-integrated manufacturing (CIM) systems within the textile industry. (http://www.citda.org)

Costume Designers Guild (CDG) is Local 892 of the International Alliance of Theatrical and Stage Employees (IATSE). The Guild represents costume designers and costume illustrators working in motion pictures, television, and commercials. It promotes the economic status of its members while improving working conditions and hosts an annual awards show. (http://www.costumedesignersguild.com)

On the Cutting Edge

Think Globally

Read domestic magazines to keep up-to-date on current developments in the field. However, do not limit your research to American magazines or ones written just in English. Many foreign fashion magazines, such as the French editions of *Elle* and *Vogue*, contain more avant-garde fashion information than domestic publications and can be a terrific source of inspiration and ideas.

Costume Society of America (CSA) advances the global understanding of all aspects of dress and appearance, and works to stimulate scholarship in the costume field. (http://www.costumesocietyamerica.com)

Council of Fashion Designers of America (CFDA) is a not-for-profit trade organization of over 300 of America's foremost fashion and accessory designers. The publicist Eleanor Lambert founded the CFDA in 1964 as a public relations tool to promote American designers to national media and to advance the status of fashion design as a branch of American art and culture. In addition to hosting the annual CFDA Fashion awards, the organization is committed to nurturing the development of the American fashion industry's future designers by supporting them in the early stages and throughout their careers. (http://www.cfda.com)

The Fashion Association (TFA) was previously called the Men's Fashion Association of America (MFA); today this organization is the nonprofit public relations arms of the apparel industry. (http://www.thefashionassociation.org)

Fashion Group International (FGI) is a global, nonprofit professional association of women executives who represent every segment of the fashion industry including apparel, accessories, beauty, and home. This 75-year-old organization was co-founded by Eleanor Roosevelt and boasts a networking body of 5,000 members, both women and men. FGI aims to be the preeminent authority on the business of fashion and design and to help its members be more effective in their careers. They sponsor an annual Career Day and a Student Design Competition. (http://www.newyork.fgi.org)

Garment Industry Development Association (GIDC) is a non-profit organization established in 1984 by the City of New York, the Garment Workers' Union (now UNITE HERE!), and the New York Skirt & Sportswear Association to strengthen New York City's apparel industry. The organization presents the views of New York's apparel manufacturing sector to the government, the press, and to industry interest groups. (http://gidc.org)

Gen Art originally operated from founder Ian Gerard's dorm kitchen at NYU Law School. Today Gen Art is an entertainment and arts organization with offices in New York, Chicago, Miami, Los Angeles, and San Francisco dedicated to showcasing emerging fashion designers, along with filmmakers, musicians, and visual artists. Gen Art hosts the annual Fresh Faces in Fashion show. (http://genart.org)

International Association of Clothing Designers and Executives (IACDE) is a trade organization for corporate executives and designers in the apparel and fashion accessories industry. (http://www.iacde.com)

IMG Fashion is the world's largest producer of fashion show events, fashion-related media programming, and event publication for fashion insiders. IMG also runs an international modeling agency. Fern Mallis, the queen of Mercedes-Benz Fashion Week, is senior vice president of IMG Fashion. (http://www.imgworld.com)

International Textile and Apparel Association, Inc. (ITAA) is an educational association for apparel and textile associated professionals including scholars, educators, and students. The organization's goal is to impart updated textile knowledge and offer an open forum for the interchange of members' ideas. (http://www.otaasite.org)

Men's Apparel Guild in California sponsors the annual MAGIC trade show in Las Vegas, the world's most comprehensive fashion trade event. (http://www.magiconline.com)

National Association of Fashion and Accessory Designers (NAFAD) is a noncommercial professional organization dedicated to fostering the creative talents and exploring the market possibilities of its members. The group works in collaboration with black universities and colleges to recruit and retain minorities in fashion and related programs. (http://nafaddc.org)

National Retail Federation (NRF) is the world's largest retail trade association. (http://www.nrf.com)

National Textile Association (NTA) is the oldest and largest association of fabric-forming companies, organized to promote the American textile industry. Members knit and weave fabric in the United States, supply fibers and yarns to the fabric-forming industry, and supply other materials and services to the American textile industry. (http://www.nationaltextile.org)

Textile/Clothing Technology Corporation (TC2), pronounced "TC-squared," is a not-for-profit, industry-wide organization that researches high-tech innovations in apparel production equipment and processes and helps the industry implement them. (http://www.tc2.com)

Young Menswear Association (YMA) is an organization devoted to furthering the interests of young people involved in the menswear apparel industry. The YMA raises funds to endow apparel-related college programs, sponsors scholarships, and hosts an annual award show to honor leadership in the apparel and textile industry. (http://the-yma.com)

Educational

Fashion schools exist in many places across the United States as well as internationally. You should consider attending school in a place where you are hoping to work after you graduate. If you live in a place where you do not have access to a fashion school, there are plenty of online programs available. What follows is a sampling of some of the most respected U.S. schools and programs.

"Brick-and-Mortar" Schools

Fashion Institute of Design and Merchandising (FIDM) is a private college operating four campuses in California (in Los Angeles, San Francisco, San Diego, and Orange County). FIDM offers a two-year associate arts degree, advanced study programs, and a B.S. in business management. Famous alums include Monique Lhuillier, Pamela Skaist-Levy, the co-founder of Juicy Couture, and Leanne Marshall, the Season 5 winner of *Project Runway*. (http://www.fidm.edu)

Fashion Institute of Technology (FIT) is a four-year public school (part of SUNY) in Manhattan. It is the world's largest fashion school. FIT offers undergraduate and graduate (master's) degrees, and graduates are placed at entry-level positions at top design studios. The Museum at FIT includes important collections of clothing, textiles, and accessories. Notable alumni of FIT include Calvin Klein, Norma Kamali, Nina Garcia, Ken Downing, Michael Kors, and Nanette Lepore. (http://www.fitnyc.edu)

Otis College of Art and Design is a Los Angeles-based college, generally referred to as Otis, which offers BFA and MFA programs as well as courses in continuing education. (http://www.otis.edu)

Parsons School of Design is part of the New School University. Parson offers undergraduate and graduate degrees as well as continuing education programs. Alumni include Patrick Robinson, Donna Karan, Mark Jacobs, Narciso Rodriguez, James Mischka, and Mark Badgley. (http://www.parsons.edu)

Pratt Institute is located in Brooklyn, New York. Pratt's Fashion Design Department is part of its School of Art and Design. The school offers a BFA in Fashion Design. (http://www.pratt.edu)

Online Fashion Programs

The Academy of Art University was founded in San Francisco in 1929. The Academy of Art University offers the following online degree programs: Bachelor of Fine Arts (BFA), Master of Fine Arts (MFA), Associate of Fine Arts (AFA), Award of Completion for Fashion design, and Award of Completion for Fashion Merchandising. (http://online.academyart.edu/fashiondesign.html)

International Academy of Design and Technology offers an online Bachelor of Arts degree program in fashion merchandising. (http://www.online.academy.edu)

Parsons School of Design offers an online degree program in fashion marketing. (http://www.newschool.edu/fmonline)

Westwood College offers an online program where you can earn a bachelor's degree in business administration with a major in fashion merchandising. (http://www.westwood.edu)

Books and Periodicals

These books can help give you a solid grounding in the history of the industry, as well as provide career advice and inspiration. Stay current with industry trends through the study of magazines, periodicals, and trade dailies.

Books

Biographies

Atlas of Fashion Designers. By Laura Eceiza (Rockport Publishers, 2009). A relevant and useful reference that maps out the complex world of contemporary fashion, featuring designers with a wide array of visions.

Chanel: A Woman of Her Own. By Axel Madsen (Henry Holt & Company, 1991). This biography of Gabrielle "Coco" Chanel examines the life and career of the woman who single-handedly changed the course of fashion.

Confessions of a Window Dresser: Confessions of a Life in Fashion. By Simon Doonan (Penguin Studio, 1998). An entertaining and irreverent romp through the author's career as a window dresser at Barneys New York, which also contains some hilarious yet sage advice for anyone contemplating work in this profession.

Front Row: Anna Wintour: What Lies Beneath the Chic Exterior of Vogue's Editor in Chief. By Jerry Oppenheimer (St. Martins Press, 2006). Based on interviews with present and former colleagues, *Front Row* tells the story of Wintour's rise to the pinnacle of fashion fame.

Ralph Lauren: The Inspiration of Four Decades. By Ralph Lauren (Random House, 2007). A fashion monograph by the architect of the American lifestyle. The famed designer introduces readers to his life, discusses his many sources of inspiration, and displays his most important, most iconic, and favorite work handpicked from hundreds of runway shows, collections, and ad campaigns. The book also includes a detailed chronology of Lauren's career and achievements.

Stylemakers: Inside Fashion. By Marcia Sherrill and Carey Adina Karmel (Monacelli Press, 2002). The authors look at the prophets, gurus, and players whose names are not recognized like those of top designers, but who play critical roles behind the scenes in today's fashion industry.

Madeleine Vionnet. By Betty Kirke with a foreword by Issey Miyake. (Chronicle Books, 1998). Vionnet was famous for her innovations with the bias cut. She created garments for many of the glamorous movie stars of the 1930s and invented new techniques of pattern making. This study of her work and legacy contains 38 original patterns for Vionnet dresses.

General Career Reference

***The Business of Fashion: Designing, Manufacturing, and Marketing,* 2nd ed.** By Leslie Davis Burns, Nancy O. Bryant (Fairchild Books, 2001). A comprehensive introduction to the business of fashion guides the reader through each step in the process of creating and marketing apparel.

***Careers for Fashion Plates and Other Trendsetters,* 3rd ed.** By Lucia Mauro (McGraw-Hill, 2008). Suggestions and strategies for finding a career in fashion, which includes information on salaries, working conditions, and opportunities for advancement.

Creative Careers in Fashion. By Debbie Hartsog (Allworth Press, 2007). This guide focuses on the most creative jobs in the fashion business, grouped in the categories of Design and Development, Merchandising, and Media and Visual Talent, and includes interviews with creative business owners and entrepreneurs.

Fashion: The Industry and Its Careers. By Michele Granger (Fairchild Books, 2007). An introduction to a wide range of jobs in this industry and how they relate to one another, as well as prospects for the future.

***Fashion Brands: Branding Style from Armani to Zara,* 2nd ed.** By Mark Tungate (London: Kogan Page, 2008). Journalist Mark Tungate had no experience in the fashion business when he started this book, but he drew on interviews and research to produce this excellent overview of the industry, written in a witty and readable style, showing how marketing and brand strategies can turn clothes and accessories into objects of desire.

***Fashion Careers: The Complete Job Search Workbook,* 4th ed.** By Wendy Samuel, Renee Palmer, and Beth Phillips (Fashion Careers, 2008). Designed as an interactive manual to guide the job seeker through all aspects of the search process, this workbook includes worksheets for self-evaluation and résumé development forms, as well as samples of résumés, cover letters, etc.

Fashion Illustrator: Drawing and Presentation for the Fashion Designer. By Bethan Morris (Abrams Studio, 2006). This useful and well-designed guide includes interviews with many established illustrators as well as tutorials in a variety of media, both traditional and computerized.

Fashion Inside Out: Daniel V's Guide to How Style Happens. By Daniel Vosovic (Watson-Guptill Publications, 2008). This excellent look inside the fashion industry is written by one of the finalists from Season 2 of the designers' competition Project Runway. Includes interviews with fashion insiders, secrets of the trade, and the unique perspective of a young and successful designer who is navigating this changing industry.

The Ins and Outs of the Fashion Industry—from a Fashion Insider. By Yolanda Brunson-Sarrabo (iUniverse, 2005). This book is like having a savvy friend in the fashion industry who takes you under her wing and offers you the benefits of her experience. Includes examples industry résumés, tips for networking, and a detailed description of New York City's Garment District.

Portfolio Presentation for Fashion Designers. By Linda Tain (Fairchild Books and Visuals, 1998). An excellent resource for anyone in the field of fashion or textile design. Shows how to create portfolios for a variety of markets, such as men's, children's, and accessories. Highly recommended.

Spark Your Career in Fashion. By Angie Wojak (Spark Publishing, 2007). This guide is specifically targeted toward college graduates looking to get a foot in the door of the fashion industry. Contains plenty of useful information about internships, networking, and office politics, and included a career-planning workbook.

Vault Career Guide to the Fashion Industry, **2nd ed.** By Holly Han (Vault, Inc, 2003). A breakdown of different jobs in fashion, with detailed looks at the typical days of people employed in the industry.

History

The American Look: Sportswear, Fashion, and the Image of Women in 1930s and 1940s New York. By Rebecca Arnold (I.B. Taurus, 2008). In this beautifully illustrated book, Arnold traces the growth of the sportswear industry and the emergence of a distinct New York fashion style during the years between the two world wars.

A Cultural History of Fashion in the Twentieth Century: From the Catwalk to the Sidewalk. By Bonnie English (Berg Publishers, 2007). This book explores the complex and fascinating history of twentieth-century fashion as forms of cultural expression and poses questions about the future of fashion as well.

The Encyclopedia of Fashion. By Georgina O'Hara (Harry N. Abrams, 1986). This illustrated encyclopedia covers the period from the 1840s through the mid-1980s in an A-Z format and presents a wide spectrum of information related to fashion.

***The End of Fashion: How Marketing Changed the Clothing Business
Forever.*** By Teri Agins (HarperCollins, 2000). Written by one of
the most well-respected reporters in the business, this fascinating book reveals the complexities of the industry and examines
the factors that ended the reign of Paris haute couture as fashion
arbiter to the world. Agins explains why designers now pour their
creativity into marketing clothes instead of designing them.

***The Fashion Cycle: A Behind-the-Scenes Look at a Year with Bill
Blass, Liz Claiborne, Donna Karan, Arnold Scassi, and Adri-
enne Vittadini.*** By Irene Daria (Simon & Schuster, 1990). Daria
is a fashion editor and journalist who gained access to these top
designers and their staff. Her book allows the reader a fly-on-wall
view of these designers and the processes by which they bring
their fashions to the consumer. Gives the reader a close-up view
of what it is like to work in the upper echelons of the industry.

Fairchild Encyclopedia of Fashion Accessories. By Phyllis G. Tortora
(Fairchild Books, 2003). This reference provides a broad overview of contemporary fashion accessories.

Fairchild Encyclopedia of Menswear. By Mary Lisa Gavenas (Fairchild Books, 2007). A comprehensive resource on the subject of
menswear for fashion students and professionals.

Fashion, Italian Style. By Valerie Steele (Yale University Press,
2003). Another excellent book by the Harold Bloom of the fashion industry. The text accompanied the exhibit organized by the
Fashion Institute of Technology in partnership with the Italian
Trade Commission (ICE).

Fifty Years of Fashion: New Look to Now. By Valerie Steele (Yale
University Press, 1997). This book was produced to accompany
an exhibition held at the Fashion Institute of Technology in New
York, and includes text by respected fashion writer and museum
director Valerie Steele that surveys the history of twentieth-
century fashion in its cultural and historical context.

Historical Dictionary of the Fashion Industry. By Francesca Sterlacci
and Joanne Arbuckle (Scarecrow Press, 2007). This useful and
comprehensive resource features information about "the events,
innovations, people, and companies that helped shape the fashion industry as we know it today" along with capsule histories
of retail giants and famous brands and definitions of industry
terminology.

History of Twentieth-Century Fashion. By Elizabeth Ewing, revised
by Alice Mackrell (Quite Specific Media Group, Limited, 2002).

Considered required reading for all those interested in the development of the fashion business, this volume focuses in particular upon the commercial development of the industry.

Icons of Fashion: The Twentieth Century. Edited by Gerda Buxbaum (Prestel, 1999). A comprehensive survey of the major fashion stories of the century, with essays by a range of savvy commentators.

In an Influential Fashion: An Encyclopedia of Nineteenth- and Twentieth-Century Fashion Designers and Retailers Who Transformed Dress. By Ann T. Kellogg, Amy T. Peterson, Stefani Bay, and Natalie Swindell (Greenwood Press, 2002). This book contains useful appendices that arrange designers and retailers by decade, country, and specialty.

In Vogue: The Illustrated History of the World's Most Famous Fashion Magazine. By Norberto Angeletti and Alberto Oliva (Rizzoli, 2006). As big and generously illustrated as the magazine itself, this comprehensive review covers everything from how *Vogue's* celebrated editors and superb photographers continue to shape the look and contents of the magazine to how it mirrors and influences the changing times.

Key Moments in Fashion. By Nigel Cawthorne, et al. (Hamlyn, 1998). Well-illustrated volume organized into chapters like "Chanel and Sunbathing" and "Anti-fashion and Punk Couture."

The Model as Muse: Embodying Fashion. By Kohle Yohannen (Yale University Press, 2009). This glossy and admiring book explores fashion's reciprocal relationship to iconic beauties that represent the evolution of the feminine ideal since the early twentieth century.

Twentieth Century Fashion. By Valerie Mendes and Amy De La Havre (Thames & Hudson, 1999). A chronologically structured survey that concentrates on significant factual aspects of the evolution of twentieth-century fashion. Focuses on international movements and highlights works by innovators from each period.

Technical References

Basics Fashion Design: Construction. By Anette Fischer (AVA Publishing, 2009). A guide to the essential stages of creating a garment that includes theory, practical skills, and techniques.

Basics Fashion Design: Developing a Collection. By Elinor Renfrew and Colin Renfrew (AVA Publishing, 2009). Teaches the process of developing a collection from initial design ideas through the development of the product to the final outcome and its ultimate exhibition and sale. Includes an overview of fashion collections through the eyes of prominent fashion journalists.

Basics Fashion Design: Research and Design. By Simon Seivewright (AVA Publishing, 2007). This guide leads readers through the essential stages of fashion research, then explains how to translate that research into design ideas.

Basics Fashion Design: Textiles and Fashion. By Jenny Udale (Ava Publishing, 2008). An authoritative overview of fabrics and techniques for dyeing, printing, embellishing, embroidering, and more. Includes case studies from textile and fabric designers.

The Dressmaker's Technique Bible. By Lorna Knight (WI:KP Books, 2008). A complete resource for designing and making clothes, which includes an at-a-glance guide to basic garment shapes and styles.

The Entrepreneur's Guide to Sewn Product Manufacturing. By Kathleen Fasanella (Apparel Technical Services, 1998). Often described as the garment industry "blue book," this practical guide is full of useful information and is highly recommended for anyone thinking about starting an apparel business.

Fashion Artist: Drawing Techniques to Portfolio Presentation. By Sandra Burke (Partners Publishers Group, 2006). Helps train the reader in key techniques of fashion drawing and design and demonstrates the accepted design standards used in the fashion industry. Used as a textbook in fashion courses but could also be part of a self-learning program.

Fashion Design, 2nd ed. By Sue Jenkyn Jones (Watson-Guptill Publications, 2005). A primer on the industry for the twenty-first century, that brings together history, theory, and practice. Includes information on how to build a collection and a portfolio and affords the reader an inside view of the industry today.

The Fashion Designer Survival Guide. By Mary Gehlhar (Kaplan Publishing, 2008). An industry insider, Gehlhar offers a comprehensive overview of the business of fashion, with advice on how to create a business plan, best sources for fabric and materials, how to navigate production problems in the United States and overseas, how to market your project and woo the press. The book includes a forward by Diane Von Furstenberg, famed designer and president of the CFDA.

The Fashion Designer's Directory of Shape and Style: Over 500 Mix-and-Match Elements for Creative Clothing Design. By Simon Travers-Spencer and Zarida Zaman (Barron's Educational Services, Inc., 2008). A profusely illustrated idea book for both professional designers and students.

***Fashion From Concept to Consumer,* 9th ed.** By Gini Stephens Frings (Prentice Hall, 2007). This a textbook but it does not read like one. As the title suggests, Frings takes the reader through the entire fashion process. The book is organized according to the design and marketing processes of the industry, and each chapter contains a career focus, chapter objectives, questions for review, and more. This edition also includes information about globalization and manufacturing technologies.

***Inside Fashion Design,* 5th ed.** By Sharon Lee Tate (Prentice Hall, 2003). An insider's view of the business and creative aspects of designing apparel. Includes information about computer-aided design (CAD) and production, resources for researching trends, as well as exercises and discussion questions to reinforce learning.

***Textiles,* 10th ed.** By Sara J. Kadolph (Prentice Hall, 2006). Provides a basic knowledge of textile production and performance. This text approaches textiles from a product analysis approach, using professional terminology, and provides examples to illustrate key concepts.

***The World of Fashion,* 4th ed.** By Jay Diamond and Ellen Diamond (Fairchild Books, 2007). An essential resource for anyone seeking to understand the fashion industry, which covers in depth the various segments of the fashion apparel and textiles industries.

The World of Fashion Merchandising. By Mary Wolfe (Goodheart-Willcox Company, Inc., 2002). An introductory text to the

Fast Facts

Create Your Own Blog!

Anybody can be a blogger. Some of the most popular fashion blogs have been created by fashionistas and style-conscious individuals with no official connections to the fashion industry, but whose blogs attracted the attention of fashion professionals. Online publishing tools from sites such as wordpress.com and Google's blogger.com can help get you started.

business aspects of the fashion world that presents the basics of market economics, textiles, design, and promotion, and offers a view of the entire textile/apparel/retail soft goods chain. Also includes advice on how to find work and succeed in the fashion industry.

The Why of the Buy: Consumer Behavior and Fashion Marketing. By Patricia Mink Rath, Stefani Bay, and Richard Petrizzi (Fairchild Books, 2008). This textbook examines how current knowledge of consumer behavior applies to the fields of fashion and design. Chapter-opening vignettes place the topics explored in each chapter in real-world settings that the reader can relate to.

Writing for the Fashion Business. By Kristen K. Swanson and Judith C. Everett (Fairchild Books, 2008). This text presents techniques for effective written communication across the whole spectrum of the fashion industry, including writing content for the Web. Includes real-world examples, case studies, and industry profiles.

Source Books

Le Book is the contact-information bible for the fashion and advertising industries. Available in New York, Paris, and London editions, this is a Who's Who of creative talent and how to reach them. Since editions currently cost $250, you may want to search for a copy at the office or in a design school library. Covers of these collectable editions have been designed by fashion luminaries such as Karl Lagerfeld, Yves Saint Laurent, Azzedine Alaia, and Vivienne Westwood. (http://www.lebook.com/gb)

Periodicals

Magazines

Elle is monthly magazine covering women's fashion, beauty, health, and entertainment. Currently the world's largest fashion magazine, with 39 international editions in over 60 countries. (http://www.elle.com)

Esquire is a monthly men's magazine published in the United States with a reputation for nurturing young writing talent. The Big Black Book, issued in the spring and fall, is a style manual for men created by the editors of *Esquire.* (http://www.esquire.com)

Essence is the first monthly magazine for African American women. It covers fashion, lifestyle, and beauty. (http://www.essence.com)

Glamour is a monthly fashion magazine currently refreshing its brand and generating a lot of positive feedback with its use of plus-sized models. (http://www.glamour.com)

GQ was originally *Gentlemen's Quarterly*. *GQ* is an upscale monthly men's magazine that covers fashion, style, and culture. (http://www.gq.com)

Harper's Bazaar is a long-running monthly fashion magazine that has had a remarkable series of editors, including Diana Vreeland and Carmel Snow. The magazine's Runway Report comes out during Fashion Week. (http://www.harpersbazaar.com)

InStyle is a monthly women's fashion magazine offering articles about beauty, fashion, home, entertaining, charity events, and celebrity lifestyles. *InStyle* also runs a companion Web site. (http://www.instyle.com)

Marie Claire is a monthly women's magazine originally conceived in France; the U.S. edition has been published since 1994. In addition to fashion information, the magazine informs readers about different women around the world and the issues they face. (http://www.marieclaire.com)

Vogue is the world's most influential fashion magazine. It is edited by Anna Wintour, the most powerful woman in fashion today. (http://www.vogue.com)

W is a monthly American fashion magazine published by Condé Nast with an oversized format. *W* covers American and European society and often likes to court controversy. It is the sister publication of *Women's Wear Daily*. (http://www.wmagazine.com)

Newspapers and Trade Publications

Apparel News is a trade paper that covers the apparel and textile industries on the West Coast.

California Apparel News provides in-depth weekly coverage of the California apparel industry, including information on trade shows, technology, and sourcing.

The Daily is awaited with baited breath by industry insiders during New York Fashion Week. Editor in chief Brandusa Niro's gossipy daily has been described as the "breathless, tongue-in-cheek love child of *Vogue* and a teen magazine."

Daily News Record (DNR) is the menswear version of WWD. DNR is published weekly and reports on the textile and menswear industries.

The Fashion Reporter is an *Entertainment Weekly* for the fashion world.

Footwear News is a weekly for the international footwear community.

The Tobe Report is an international weekly publication that covers women's, men's, and children's ready-to-wear and accessories. It forecasts trends through analysis of consumer behavior and retail data.

Women's Wear Daily (WWD) is considered essential reading in the industry. WWD is the daily trade paper that covers international news of the fashion, beauty, and retail industries.

Other Media: Films

Here are few films where fashion takes center stage. You will likely have your own favorites to add to this list.

American Gigolo (1980) put Giorgio Armani on the fashion radar of American men by featuring his suits as worn by Richard Gere.

Breakfast at Tiffany's (1961) established the little black dress as a fashion must, featuring fashions by Edith Head, Hubert de Givenchy, and Pauline Trigère.

The Devil Wears Prada (2006) stars Meryl Streep as Miranda Priestly, the Anna Wintour-like boss from hell, and Anne Hathaway as her beleaguered assistant.

Funny Face (1957) stars Audrey Hepburn as Jo Stockton, a bookstore salesgirl who becomes a fashion model. Fred Astaire plays Dick Avery (based on real-life cameraman Richard Avedon), who discovers her.

Picture Me: A Model's Diary (2009) is a documentary by Sarah Ziff about treatment of models in the fashion industry.

Prêt-à-Porter (1994) is a satirical comedy by the late, great Robert Altman about a fashion show in Paris. It was shot during Fashion Week with a host of international stars, models, and designers. The film's most famous scene occurs at the end when nude female models stride along the catwalk.

The September Issue (2009) is a fascinating documentary that chronicles *Vogue* editor in chief Anna Wintour's preparations for the 2007 fall-fashion issue, which promises to be the biggest one ever. At the center of the action is the working relationship between Wintour and Grace Coddington, creative director of the magazine.

Best Practice

Build a Web Site

An aspiring fashion photographer needs to have a great portfolio, naturally. If you want to be taken seriously as a photographer today you will also need to establish your own Web site to promote your work. Formerly, you had to pay a Web designer to put a site together for you, which could get pretty pricey. Today there are a growing number of reasonably priced sites such as Viewbook and Cliqbook that will let you create a professional-looking site to house your images for a reasonable annual fee.

Unzipped (1995) is a very entertaining documentary about the fashion designer Isaac Mizrahi that offers a hilarious and revealing look at the high-powered world of fashion.

Web Sites

Fashion and the Internet seem to be made for each other. The speed at which information can be shared with users around the world has changed forever the way that the industry works, and social networks like Twitter are paving the way for trends to come and go with lightning speed. How this will all affect the future of fashion remains to be seen, but here are some great sites worth visiting:

Apparel Search is an apparel industry online directory providing members of the fashion community with links to all aspects of the trade, including jobs, news, financial information, and much more. Includes a business-to-business directory. (http://www.apparelsearch.com)

Bobbin.com is the business and technology authority for the sewn products industry. (http://www.bobbin.com)

The Costume Institute at the Metropolitan Museum of Art is a collection of more than 30,000 costumes and accessories, many available to search and view online. (http://www.metmuseum.org/Work_of_Art/the_costume_institute)

Garmento.org is a Web resource for apparel, garment, and fashion manufacturers, designers, models, and home sewers. (http://www.garmento.org)

Ecofashionworld.com is a Web site covering eco-fashion and ethical fashion news from around the world. Features an organic and ethical fashion guide and sustainable clothing brand directory. (http://www.ecofashionworld.com)

Fabriclink.com is a consumer resource providing information on fabrics, apparel, and home furnishings. Includes a textile dictionary and a fabric care center among other useful features. (http://www.Fabriclink.com/Dictionaries/Textile.cfm)

The Fashion Calendar is an authoritative listing of national and international fashion events. This calendar enables designers and manufacturers to keep up-to-date with market weeks and avoid scheduling conflicts. The Fashion Calendar has been an industry resource for more than 50 years. (http://www.fashioncalendar.net)

The Fashion Center is the source for New York fashion industry information. (http://www.fashioncenter.com)

Fashionoffice.org is an online magazine covering fashion, beauty, and lifestyle news. (http://www.fashionoffice.org)

Fashion Wire Daily is a syndicated wire service covering designer collections, celebrity style, entertainment, fitness, beauty, lifestyle, and home. (http://www.fashionwiredaily.com)

Genart.com is a fashion competition for anyone. New designers can download an application. Genart hosts an annual runway show called "Fresh Faces in Fashion" that showcases up to eight emerging designers and four accessories designers in standing installations. Genart has helped launch the careers of designers such as Zac Posen, Shoshanna, Chaiken, and others. Styles International Design Competition assembles a group of 30 industry professionals (editors and retail buyers) to chose 25 finalists whose looks will be presented at the Style event, for a chance to win one of five $5,000 Awards for Design Excellence. Previous winners include Rodarte, Jeffrey Chow, and Cloak. Visit for competition guidelines. (http://discover.genart.org)

Models.com is a free service for models, makeup artists, and photographers. (http://www.models.com)

The Museum at the Fashion Institute of Technology holds one of the world's most important collections of costume and textiles, with particular strength in twentieth-century fashion. You can

access images of this terrific collection online. (http://www.fitnyc
.edu/museum)

Promostyl is a trend forecasting agency. (http://www.promostyl
.com)

Trendzine is a women's wear forecast and trend-reporting service
offering detailed insight into European fashion trends. (http://
www.fashioninformation.com)

Index